The Small Museum Toolkit, Book 5

The Small Museum Toolkit, Book 5

Interpretation: Education, Programs, and Exhibits

Edited by
Cinnamon Catlin-Legutko
and Stacy Klingler

ALTAMIRA
PRESS

A division of
ROWMAN & LITTLEFIELD PUBLISHERS, INC.
Lanham • New York • Toronto • Plymouth, UK

Published by AltaMira Press
A division of Rowman & Littlefield Publishers, Inc.
A wholly owned subsidiary of The Rowman & Littlefield Publishing Group, Inc.
4501 Forbes Boulevard, Suite 200, Lanham, Maryland 20706
http://www.altamirapress.com

Estover Road, Plymouth PL6 7PY, United Kingdom

British Library Cataloguing in Publication Information Available

Library of Congress Cataloging-in-Publication Data

The small museum toolkit. Book 5, Interpretation : education, programs, and exhibits / edited by Cinnamon Catlin-Legutko and Stacy Klingler.
    p. cm. — (American Association for State and Local History book series)
  Includes bibliographical references and index.
  ISBN 978-0-7591-1952-9 (cloth : alk. paper) — ISBN 978-0-7591-1339-8 (pbk. : alk. paper) — ISBN 978-0-7591-1346-6 (electronic)
  1. Small museums—Exhibitions. 2. Communication in museums. 3. Interpretation of cultural and natural resources. I. Catlin-Legutko, Cinnamon. II. Klingler, Stacy, 1976– III. Title: Interpretation.
  AM125.S63 2012
  069.5—dc23   2011028448

♾™ The paper used in this publication meets the minimum requirements of American National Standard for Information Sciences—Permanence of Paper for Printed Library Materials, ANSI/NISO Z39.48-1992.

Printed in the United States of America

CONTENTS

EDITORS' NOTE

Small museums are faced with the enormous task of matching the responsibilities of a large museum—planning strategically, securing and managing human and financial resources, providing stewardship of collections (including historic buildings) as well as excellent exhibitions, programs, and publications, and responding to changing community and visitor needs—all with more limited human and financial resources. Small museum staff (paid or unpaid) often fulfill key responsibilities outside their area of expertise or training.

We recognize that small museum staff lack time more than anything. To help you in the trenches, we offer this quick reference, written with your working environment in mind, to make the process of becoming a sustainable, valued institution less overwhelming.

The Small Museum Toolkit is designed as a single collection of short, readable books that provides the starting point for realizing key responsibilities in museum work. Each book stands alone, but as a collection they represent a single resource to jump-start the process of pursing best practices and meeting museum standards.

If you are new to working in museums, you may want to read the entire series to get the lay of the land—an overview of what issues you should be aware of and where you can find resources for more information. If you have some museum training but are now responsible for more elements of museum operations than in your previous position, you may start with just the books or chapters covering unfamiliar territory. (You might be wishing you had taken a class in fundraising right about now!) As you prepare to tackle new challenges, we hope that you will refer back to a chapter to orient yourself.

While any chapter can be helpful if read in isolation, we suggest that you start with the first book, *Leadership, Mission, and Governance*, and look at the issues of mission, planning, and assessment. You will find that almost every chapter asks you to consider its subject in light of your mission and make decisions based on it. As you begin to feel overwhelmed by all the possible opportunities and challenges you face, assessment and planning will help you focus your scarce resources strategically—where you need them the most and where they can produce the biggest impact on your organization. And this book offers tips for good governance—defining the role of a trustee and managing the director-trustee relationship. Understanding this relationship from the outset will prevent many headaches down the road.

Financial Resource Development and Management offers you direction about how to raise and manage money and stay within your legal boundaries as a nonprofit. How to manage resources, human and inanimate, effectively and efficiently is discussed in *Organizational Management*. *Reaching and Responding to the Audience* encourages you to examine your museum audiences and make them comfortable, program to their needs and interests, and spread the word about your good work.

The remaining two books explore the museum foundational concepts of interpretation and stewardship in a small museum setting. *Interpretation: Education, Programs, and Exhibits* considers researching and designing exhibits and best practices for sharing the stories with your audiences. *Stewardship: Collections and Historic Preservation* rounds out the six-book series with an in-depth look at collections care, management, and planning.

We would like to thank the staff at the American Association for State and Local History and AltaMira Press, our families, and our colleagues for encouraging us to pursue this project. You have tirelessly offered your support, and we are incredibly grateful.

There is little reward for writing in service to the museum field—and even less time to do it when you work in a small museum. The contributors to this series generously carved time out of their work and personal lives to share with you their perspectives and lessons learned from years of experience. While not all of them currently hang their hats in small museums, every one of them has worked with or for a small museum and values the incredible work small museums accomplish every day. We offer each and every one of them more appreciation than we can put into words.

We hope that this series makes your lives—as small museum directors, board members, and paid and unpaid staff members—just a little bit easier. We hope that we have gathered helpful perspectives and pointed you in the direction of useful resources.

And when you are faced with a minor annoyance, a major disaster, or just one too many surprises, remember why you do this important work and that you are not alone.

It takes a very special kind of person to endure and enjoy this profession for a lifetime. Not a day passes in which I do not learn something, or find something, or teach something, or preserve something, or help someone.

—Unknown author

Keep up the good work!

Cinnamon Catlin-Legutko
Stacy Lynn Klingler
Editors

PREFACE

I have a confession to make. Until I got to the American Association for State and Local History (AASLH), I never truly understood what it was to work in a small museum. Sure, I had been around them, visited them, talked to my peers who worked in them both as paid and unpaid (read: volunteer) staff, and appreciated the role they play in the historical narrative and in communities. But I never *got it* until I got to AASLH.

So what have I learned? First and foremost, small museums are the bedrock of the American museum profession. You will not find museums the size of the Smithsonian or historic sites like Gettysburg in every American community, but you will often find a small museum, sometimes more than one. While we in the historical profession talk often about how we are the keepers of the American past, and we are, those who work in the smaller institutions are truly minders of our nation's patrimony and heritage. They care for the objects and history of communities throughout the country, stories that would probably be lost without that care. Quite simply, without small museums, our knowledge of the past, our historical narrative, would be incomplete.

The second thing I have learned, and been truly humbled by, is the passion and dedication small museum professionals and volunteers have for their craft. You will rarely hear small museum professionals complaining about a lack of resources—that is just part and parcel of the task at hand. Instead of attacking a challenge with reasons for why something cannot be done, they redirect their thoughts to how it can be done within the parameters provided. So, small museum professionals are equally comfortable with answering the phone, giving a tour, processing collections, and plunging the occasional toilet (the latter falling into the "other duties as assigned" category in a job description).

And amid all that, small museum professionals keep a great sense of humor. At several gatherings of small museum folks over the years, we have had fun with a game we call "You Know You Work in a Small Museum If . . ." Responses ranged from "A staff meeting consists of all staff members turning around in their office chairs at the same time" to "You're the director, but if you're the first one to work after a snowstorm, you get to shovel the sidewalk and plow the parking lot." But my absolute favorite was "When you walk through the gallery and hear a guest say, 'The staff should really do . . .' and you think, Hey, *I'm* my staff!"

At one time, as Steve Friesen of the Buffalo Bill Museum and Grave notes in chapter 2 of Book 1 of this series, the term *small museum* was used as a pejorative. Small museums were underfunded, under-resourced, and poorly managed. "If they weren't," the thinking went, "they'd be large museums, right?" Wrong. Being small does not mean you aspire to be big or that the institution is small because it is doing something wrong. Smallness has more to do with a spirit and dedication to a certain niche of history, a community, a person, a subject.

I believe the field has moved beyond that prejudice, and small museums are now celebrated. At AASLH we often discuss how much larger museums can learn from smaller institutions about how to serve as effective stewards of their resources and to engage their communities in a deep, meaningful way. There is much to learn from small museums, and our peers and colleagues at those institutions are ever willing to share.

Along this line, I have always found that one of the best things about the museum profession in general is how open it is with regard to sharing ideas and processes and just offering support. In no corner of the field is this more evident than in the world of small museums. Small museum professionals are founts of wisdom and expertise, and every small museum session, luncheon, or affinity event I have been to has been packed, and discussion has been stimulating and often inspiring. In fact, discussion often spills out into the hallways after the formal session has concluded.

But the work I know best is that of the AASLH Small Museums Committee. The editors of this series, Cinnamon Catlin-Legutko and Stacy Klingler, are, respectively, the founding and current chairs of this committee. Under their leadership, a team of small museum folks has completed a set of ambitious goals, including gathering a variety of research and developing a small museum needs assessment, presenting sessions at conferences throughout the country, and raising money for scholarships to send peers to the AASLH annual meeting each year. It is this last item I want to highlight as it gives the clearest example of the love and commitment those in small museums have for each other.

In my view, the fact that the Small Museums Committee successfully organizes an annual fundraising campaign is commendable. The fact that it routinely raises money to send *two* people to the meeting (and four people in some years) is truly remarkable. This is indicative of the passion and dedication small museum professionals feel toward the cause of small museums and toward their colleagues. Let's face it, history professionals are not at the top of the salary food chain. (I always note this whenever I speak to history classes about a career in public history. "If you choose this career, you are going to love what you do; you are going to be making a difference in your community. But you are also taking a vow of poverty. No one goes into the history field to get rich.") And while donors to this fund are not all from small museums, small museum professionals are a large part of the pool, giving as generously as anyone. I am so heartened each year as we raise this money.

So, what does all this have to do with the book in your hands? I would say a lot. First, the contributors are small museum professionals or aficionados themselves. They are dedicated to the craft in the small museum environment and know firsthand its needs and challenges. In addition, they have been involved with, and led national discussions on, these issues. They are passionate about the cause of small museums, and they have organized and written a book (and series) that offers a variety of voices and contexts while speaking to the needs as articulated. The thirty-plus contributors to this series offer a wealth of experience and expertise in dealing with the complex nature of running a small museum, in preserving traces of the American past for future generations, often on a shoestring budget and with limited resources. It is a lesson we can all learn. And it is a lesson well articulated here.

Whether you are a seasoned small museum professional, a newly minted executive director, or a museum studies or public history student, it is my hope that this book series will give you the tools you need to succeed in your job. I also hope that you will continue to carry the torch for small museums in your community and in the larger museum field. The field needs your passion and expertise, and the role you fill in your community is critical.

Bob Beatty
Vice President, AASLH

PREPARING AN OUTSTANDING CONCERT: HOW TO PLAN AND IMPLEMENT INTERPRETATION

Stephen G. Hague and Laura C. Keim[1]

Interpretation is, at its core, communication. Buildings, landscapes, works of art, and other artifacts in collections have things to tell us. They are physical stand-ins, or representatives, for the people who may have made, owned, used, or discovered them. It is up to us, the interpreters of collections, to provide information about the objects in our museums and their context in order to encourage a process of discovery. Our job is to understand some of what objects have to say and, in turn, to offer those meanings and messages to museum visitors in a thought-provoking and engaging way, whether through guided tours, exhibits, or other programs. Interpretation is explanation and a form of translation, making the elusive languages, or "melodies," of the objects perceptible and understandable to the audience.[2]

This chapter focuses on planning and developing interpretation in your museum (a.k.a. interpretive planning), training staff and volunteers to understand and implement interpretive ideas, and executing tours in museums. Interpretation is considered broadly. It not only entails the specific information imparted as part of a structured tour experience but can also include a range of vehicles for delivering this information. This chapter highlights that the best small museums

- make a strong strategic commitment to audience-centered interpretation as the primary focus of their activities;
- plan interpretation using the available resources of their site and drawing on the expertise of scholars, staff, volunteers, community members, and others;
- train staff and volunteers at all levels of the organization to impart interpretive themes in a variety of ways;
- effectively execute interpretation at all levels, evaluate the results, and make changes and adjustments.

Much of the information in this chapter is based on experience developing interpretive plans for several historic sites, as well as an interpretive framework for a consortium of fourteen organizations, including several historic houses, a historical society, an arboretum, and an art museum. At the heart of each of these processes, it was important to find the key messages that each site could best convey. Or, in the words of interpretive planning consultant Sandra Mackenzie Lloyd, we wanted to "sing the song the site sings best." This metaphor carries throughout the chapter. Although developed specifically for historic sites, the lessons and methods described are relevant to any efforts to define and develop interpretive content and can easily be applied to all small museums.

Each museum has a song to sing that constitutes its reason for being. It is in our interest to play to our strengths, or to sing the songs that we perform best. We also need, however, to retain flexibility, to be able to sing for different audiences, and to perform a range of tunes with different moods and lengths. A lot of preparation goes into the final performance. Do we do opera, jazz, or hip-hop best? In putting on the concert, what do audiences want to hear? How often should we rehearse? How do we craft an interesting program with a range of pieces? How do we train the musicians? How do we respond to the critics and make changes? This chapter seeks to offer straightforward answers to these questions.

There are many ways of conveying information about your museum in multiple contexts. Interpretation is a holistic concept that permeates every museum,

Photo 1.1. A Back of the House Tour engages with the idea that a house can be seen back-to-front as well as front-to-back, so that service spaces can get special emphasis. Here a guide describes how the outbuildings and backyard operated. (Courtesy of Historic Germantown, Philadelphia, Pennsylvania)

not necessarily restricted any longer to a coterie of guides but taking in everyone who comes into contact with the public. As museums have tried new and different strategies for reaching expanded and more diverse audiences, they have encountered a range of learning styles and visitor expectations.

As will become evident in reading other chapters in this book, tours are not the only way to impart information about your museum. Indeed, they may not be the best way. For example, visitors could be taking a self-guided tour at the summer garden party, wandering through with the children in anticipation of the Easter egg hunt, or just having a look around between sets of the jazz concert in the main gallery. All of these offer opportunities for people to explore, experience, and learn about and from your museum. You need to be ready for them all!

Deciding to Sing: Committing to Good Interpretation

Committing to offer good interpretation—making the conscious decision to sing—is the first major step in interpreting effectively. Interpretation thus needs to be the primary focus stated by the museum. This seems to be intuitive—of course we want to tell people about all the great stuff we have. But too often this focus has not been central for all museums. A major shift in accepted interpretive practice has taken place over the last decade or so. Museums have moved from being collections centered to audience centered. As Book 6 in this series addresses, this means that while preserving buildings and collections is still a vital part of what we do, conveying information about these important objects and the people represented by them is paramount.

Although there remains a great responsibility for buildings and collections, what we do with those objects matters most. Or, to put it another way, you must provide a forum that first and foremost allows people to experience and engage with your museum in a way comfortable for them. Nothing connects people to the past better than a story they can relate to; good interpretation helps us do this.

The idea of reaching various audiences needs to underpin every facet of a museum's operations. A tour begins long before you and your visitors enter the first gallery or period room. All members of the board, staff, and volunteer corps should understand and be committed to the idea that they are engaged in public service. This can be done formally through a policy document or strategic plan that clearly states the importance of interpretation, a board-approved interpretive plan that guides the staff in developing content, and a staff and volunteers trained to understand the critical importance of this part of the museum's work. It can be done informally by instituting and insisting upon an organizational culture that values high-quality interpretation and places extraordinary emphasis on accurate, open communication and interaction.

What is more, this approach can no longer only be restricted to tour guides. As fewer visitors experience museums and historic sites through the mechanism of the guided tour, the definition of interpretation has been stretched, as has the sense of who is responsible for it. No longer is a highly trained guide delivering extensive information in a structured, highly controlled format the norm. Based on audience figures for several sites in Philadelphia, Pennsylvania, an increasingly small percentage of the annual visitation is represented in the form of guided tours. Far more people are coming for events, activities, school programs, meetings, and even weddings or other special functions. All of these visitors are part of the audience. Most will have some curiosity about your museum, but they will have varying levels of interest and expectation. The goal of good interpretation is to see that your interpretive focus is reflected in every aspect of your museum operations.

This means that board, staff, and volunteers all need to be aware of and committed to the overall goal of interpreting your museum. The commitment to interpretation and public education should be made clear in policy documents, training materials, and daily operations. There should also be periodic reviews of interpretive goals—at least every five years but more frequently as needed. Regular evaluation, covered below, can serve as an indicator of how often.

Interpretation has to be at the core of every museum and become part of your organization's culture. The importance of good interpretation can easily be lost when other issues such as the leaky roof or the budget deficit take priority. But the best small museums start with the idea that they exist to offer a wide range of interpretation—tours, educational programs, workshops, exhibits, publications, even social activities—to as broad a public as possible.

To Whom Are We Singing? Knowing Your Audience

One major component of successful interpretation is audience information. Speakers are told to know their audience, and museums need to listen to this good advice. Make a concerted effort to understand your actual and potential audiences.

Before embarking on interpretive planning, or as part of the process, build in audience evaluation components. This allows the museum to gain a greater understanding of the sorts of themes that interest current visitors and might potentially interest others. This can take various forms. Survey current visitors to assess what aspects of the museum speak to them. The American Association for State and Local History (AASLH) has a survey program available for museums, as do other museum groups, or you can construct your own with the help of a local firm.[3] (Or, for more information on do-it-yourself surveys and evaluation, see chapter 2 in Book 4 of this series.) Although these programs elicit responses

CASE STUDY: THE "NEW" FRANCIS ART MUSEUM

The Francis Art Museum (FAM) had always been the "big dog" in the neighborhood. Supported in part by a prominent parent organization, the FAM was the largest local cultural institution and welcomed a significant number of visitors every year. Some came to see the paintings and objects, others to watch the annual reenactment of the Civil War battle that took place on its grounds when it was a private house. Part of the FAM was used for meetings by a few local groups, and the grounds hosted the annual town picnic. Nevertheless, a few picnic goers, when asked if they liked the FAM, responded, "Dunno, never been there."

This pointed to a problem. The FAM was physically located in the community, but it was not necessarily always part of the community fabric. In discussions with the museum's parent organization, the board and staff decided that something had to change. In order to be really successful, they needed to do some deep thinking about what they wanted FAM to be as an organization. Although this involved months of strategic planning meetings, retreats, budget discussions, and some good old-fashioned soul-searching, they came away with a commitment to the "New" Francis Art Museum. This included adopting an audience-centered interpretation that relied on community feedback and input. It involved thinking outside the box and doing innovative programs, like holding a youth writer's workshop in conjunction with a local university and using the paintings collection for inspiration. This in turn called for further community engagement, and a range of interpretive projects were undertaken with partner institutions such as schools, churches, businesses, and community groups.

When the local congressman wrote out of the blue to laud the work of FAM, it meant a great deal, but perhaps not as much as the positive response of the many first-time visitors who enjoyed looking at art while quaffing ale at the newly inaugurated FAM Beer Festival. Several years on, the Francis Art Museum had become not only a museum but also a community leader, with its attendance nearly doubled. It had made a serious and strong commitment to new interpretive practices, and this spirit now pervades all its activities. At every level, the "New" FAM believes that engaging diverse audiences in multilayered ways is the core of what it does.

from those who already visit or have an interest in your museum, they can give you a great deal of valuable information as you plan.

You can also look to analyze potential audiences. If you do not have much participation from your community, conduct focus groups with local leaders or one-on-one interviews asking them what sorts of connection they envision with your museum. Consider whether some sort of recurring activity or club might suit your mission or interpretation and could meet regularly at, and become affiliated with, your museum. Build partnerships with other organizations when possible as this holds the potential to broaden your reach and deepen your impact.

If you have a website (and every museum should), you should utilize it as a way of gathering data. This might include social networking sites and other vehicles that link your museum with the connected community of cyberspace. Although this chapter does not focus on technology, it is in the best interest of every museum to utilize technology to gather, convey, and share information.

You should not only rely on feedback from audiences about what they want to see your museum talk about and do but ask them to participate more fully in your process. Familiarize them with your site and what is special about it. Involve them in your decision-making. Solicit their advice. Better yet, act on and incorporate their ideas. People like nothing better than when they have a good idea and someone actually makes it a reality. Although this can be challenging and produce unexpected results, it is also a particularly vibrant way to give your museum and its message meaning.

Having said all this, museums must be wary of overextending. Although organizations in this day and age need to be much more responsive to a public with wide-ranging interests, small museums must play to their strengths. If you are a small science museum, collecting and interpreting works by local artists may never be on your agenda. A suggestion like this, however, might be just the sort of prompt you need to develop a program or exhibition that links these local artists with scientific themes. It could be an innovative collaboration in the making. Then again, it might not. Whatever your choice, your decision-making process will be better informed knowing to whom you are singing and what your audience wants to hear.

What Song to Sing? Development of Clear, Focused Interpretive Themes

Thoughtful planning is essential in the creation of effective interpretation. Once your organization has accepted root and branch that interpretation is your primary focus, you are ready to move on to planning what that interpretation will be. Having done the hard background work to position yourself for your singing career, it is time to decide on the repertoire.

A good interpretive plan offers key concepts and a structure designed to spin a web of connections for the visitor between what they are seeing in the museum and their own experiences and lives. Making those connections strongly will capture the visitor's imagination on a deep and resonant level. Although we cannot in every instance do this explicitly, the more connections that visitors can make to the story of your museum, the more often they will want to return and become engaged.

The interpretive planning process takes time. First, everyone in the organization must be on board, knowing that the plan will ultimately generate new ideas and approaches. It can be helpful to emphasize that the plan may only codify messages that are already part of the museum's current offerings. While an interpretive plan can be a wholesale change in how a museum approaches itself, it does not have to be. If you do not want to lose existing stakeholders while you consider strategies for building relationships with new ones, it is helpful to think of the plan as including existing messages or aspects of your interpretation that you already do well.

All interpretation must rest on the bedrock of good scholarship, so do involve scholars and other experts early and often. Engage actively with scholarship, reading new material in your field regularly. When developing interpretive planning documents, staff and volunteers should conduct their own research and build their own knowledge foundations.

At the same time, remember that you have an obligation to convey scholarship to a wide public. Academic research should support what you do, but do not let it take over. Although the postmodern discourse related to the "liminal space of the dining room table's social topography" (as one scholar opaquely commented in a planning session) may sound impressive and contain some really good nuggets of academic research, you need to play the translator. Few visitors think of table settings as "social topography," but they will understand the idea of social hierarchies and how they may be communicated through architectural space or the use of various types of tableware.

This does not mean dumbing down, in the parlance of the day. Just the opposite. You want to challenge your audience, engaging fully with difficult topics and complex ideas. As discussed in chapter 2 of this book, topics related to race, ethnicity, war, violence, immigration, enslavement, and class all belong in museums. Complicated issues or problems can have great resonance for visitors. These topics are made more tangible and meaningful when you can rely on solid, up-to-date research in crafting your interpretation.

CASE STUDY: DEVELOPING INTERPRETIVE THEMES

One interpretive planning document developed for a consortium of historic sites and museums had four key interpretive concepts. The concepts specifically incorporated the mission of each organization, with histories ranging from the eighteenth to the twentieth centuries, and connected the organizations with their surrounding communities.

The interpretive concepts had short descriptions that identified how each theme related to the individual sites. The first spoke about the enduring search for freedom in the area, the second touched upon the importance of accepting differences in a multicultural community, the third highlighted the industrious people who had created commerce and culture in the community, and the fourth highlighted the special aesthetic character of the surrounding natural and built environment. These four concepts could be summed up in short words or phrases that had resonance for the sites and the public:

- Freedom
- Acceptance
- Hard work
- Beauty

These concepts suggested nearly universal values but linked them to the histories of fourteen museums. They were easy to remember and took the histories of all the organizations into account, allowing each individual site to contribute to the whole and make strong, vibrant associations with its locale.

Establishing themes, the underlying chords and foundation for the future songs your museum will sing, is core. The themes are the key concepts and messages that your museum will convey to visitors and to participants in your programs. These themes are not proclaimed on signs or listed anywhere. No guide should ever say, "The four themes of our museum are . . ." Rather, the themes ground and permeate everything done at the museum. They help the museum to know its core identity and communicate it to the world.

An Interlude: Funding the Concert

Planning is an area where small museums are apt to skimp on the budget. There is always something seemingly more important to be done with vital and scarce resources. All museums worry about money, and in an era of tightened belts, smaller museums may worry more than others. This does not diminish the importance of interpretive planning. Rather, it forces us to be creative with how we do it.

Before setting out on this process, compile a budget. This should factor in money that will likely be spent (and there will be some of this) but, perhaps even more importantly, be clear about the time and energy that will be expended. Remember to include the costs of your staff and volunteers; good planning and training will take their time as well as money, and this should be quantified in some way. For budgets, the following may apply to your list of possible expenditures[4]:

- Staff
- Consultants
- Travel
- Meals/subsistence
- Telecommunications (telephone, website)
- Marketing/publicity
- Related programming (i.e., pilot programs)
- Printing
- Supplies and materials
- Administrative overhead

As with all things, the range of costs varies. Interpretive planning projects, especially when they are well conceived and follow the guidelines in this chapter, are compelling and can attract outside funding. All of the projects highlighted in this chapter were largely completed with grants from private or public sources, including foundations and state and national funding bodies.

If a grant or other funding is available, that can help the process, but this does not need to be costly. Excellent projects can be undertaken for a few hundred dollars, while more elaborate processes can cost tens of thousands, although with creativity they can be done for far less. Many small museums may find it easier to have a committed group of volunteers expend time and energy than to spend cash. Find ways to recruit volunteers—perhaps local teachers or an art historian from a local college. Secure donations for printing. Few organizations are as imaginative in this regard as small museums. If you are committed to this process and willing to be creative to see it through, then the budget can be scaled accordingly. A community concert done on a shoestring budget can be just as rewarding and enjoyable as one by a big-city symphony orchestra.

What Does the Song Sheet Look Like?
Creation of Written Plans

Like a group of singers, who all need music to read from, every museum should have a concise, comprehensive, and clear interpretive plan to harness their energies and focus their work. The written interpretive plan and all other documents related to interpretation, such as policies, guide manuals, training handbooks, and exhibit plans, should clearly state your key themes and concepts.

Developing themes for your museum is step one. This is ideally done in a setting that involves carefully selected insiders and outsiders, including staff, volunteers, neighbors, collaborators, advisors from other museums, and scholars. Themes should be coherent concepts; three to five are about right for most museums. If you have too many, you risk diluting what you are about. If you have less than three, you might limit the way that you engage with various topics or ideas.

If you have funding, hiring an interpretive planning consultant to guide the process helps to ensure a high level of professionalism and unburden the staff. As an example, one historic site brought together a full interpretive planning team of staff, volunteers, and consultants on-site for two meetings. For the first, all had read basic background material, which included a tour script that was then the core of standard guide training. The team toured the site at length and considered each space, taking lots of notes. After lunch, to address the question of what song the site sang best, everyone involved filled out a 3 × 5 card with one or two sentences finishing the phrase "The story of the site is . . ." The team members shared what they had written and discussed the answers. The scholars on the team went away and wrote brief essays on their area of expertise, especially as it pertained to the museum. As all this material was put together, the themes began to emerge and then informed the work of the staff and lead consultant in beginning to write the plan.

The next step is the development of a written document that sets out and builds on the themes, describing in further detail how they can be employed in a number of ways in your museum. Museums are assemblages, and the job of interpretation is to make sense of that assemblage. An interpretive plan is not a script of any kind but instead creates a framework or structure for understanding the museum, relating specific spaces, objects, and people (past and present) to each other and to larger cultural or historical ideas. Your museum contains its site-specific collections. Your goal is to set those collections—be they household objects, pieces of fine art, plants, rocks, or buildings—into a larger context that makes sense and has meaning for the public. The case study in textbox 1.3 is based on the process undertaken at one historic site. Although the process can vary from organization to organization, and all have bumps in the road, this

CASE STUDY: GARSINI HOUSE INTERPRETIVE PLAN[1]

The Garsini House knew it needed to develop an interpretive plan but did not know where to begin. It was not even quite sure what an interpretive plan was. After reading sources related to tour giving and development and talking with a host of other sites, it seemed that interpretive planning was an organized way to present information about the site, developing larger themes and connecting them with broader human experiences.

Not everyone in the organization was sure what this meant or what it would look like when it was finished. Was it a new tour script that revised the one done twenty years ago? Would it change the way people moved through the rooms in the house? Was it a way to shorten the tours, in which case Mr. Murgatroyd and that great story about Hannah saving the house from being burned by rioters in 1911 might need to be dropped? Although all these were immediate questions, the Garsini House staff decided to develop a process to assess what stories they were telling. They started by talking with a consultant, who offered ideas about how the project could be structured. Next, they created an advisory panel, which included several historians, an interpretation expert, an exhibit designer, a teacher, several members of the board, and a number of community members. With this organized, the Garsini House wrote a grant to the local Humanities Council and the ABC Foundation, which were impressed with all this forethought and provided some funding for the process.

Over the course of months, the whole group met three times, with smaller groups working on their areas in between larger meetings. Group members did a lot of research beforehand, reading up on the history of the site, asking people in the community to fill out surveys, conducting focus groups and interviews, and looking at other reports. The first brainstorming session tackled what was important about the Garsini House. Some of the historians had one answer; some community members had another; some of the teachers had a third. Over discussion at several meetings, it became clear that no matter how each person approached the Garsini House, several themes were becoming clear. These themes were broad enough to include all the views expressed but focused enough to give the site meaning to a range of audiences.

Finally, the Garsini House produced a written plan. This relatively brief document described the three themes. It also explained how those themes and

(continued)

TEXTBOX 1.3 *(Continued)*

information about the Garsini House could be imparted to visitors. A large part of this was for a guided tour, but every way the staff and advisory council could think that information might be passed along was included: brochures, signage, temporary and permanent exhibits, garden labels, websites, podcasts, videos, magazine articles, events, and programs. The interpretive plan left room for Mr. Murgatroyd and for Hannah, even allowing their stories to be told in fresh ways. After the plan was done, several new guides were given copies and were impressed by how easy the well-structured document made their training. Most importantly, the interpretive plan had responded to a range of audiences, incorporating their ideas and energy and ensuring that the Garsini House would have meaning for everyone in its community.

Note

1. To enhance their instructive value, this chapter's case study examples are fictional but based on actual small museum experiences.

process took about one year to complete, with a small staff doing much of the writing based on the work of a project team as described.

An interpretive plan provides structure and key concepts, while allowing interpreters to create tours that respond to the needs of individual visitors and groups. An interpretive plan should contain sections that address the following:

1. *Introduction:* Detail the process and introduce the document.
2. *Major themes:* Clearly lay out your main themes.
3. *Statement of interpretive philosophy:* State how these themes will be used.
4. *Museum-specific content:* Describe the stories, people, and objects related to your museum.
5. *Recommendations:* Discuss further work that might need to be done to support the museum's interpretation.

Some written interpretive plans contain more elements, but these are important features in making your plan clear and meaningful.

One way to organize the plan is to draft a one-page form including the theme, context, and background information and a chart for stories or topics, related objects, and related people. The interpretive plan for one museum offers these one-page information sheets for every space on the property: welcome and orientation areas, rooms, outbuildings, the garden, the landscape, and a graveyard. Textbox 1.4 shows a similar form for the Garsini House.

TEXTBOX 1.4

SPACE/GALLERY:
MR. MURGATROYD'S STUDY

Main Theme
Identify the main theme for the space with a brief description. This should be linked to the one of the interpretive themes, while allowing for interpretive flexibility. An example might be Mr. Murgatroyd's important political and business career. More than one theme may be mentioned. Stories, objects, and people support the theme(s). The topics or stories can be used as needed or in combination to develop a range of tours.

Topics or Stories to Discuss	Objects Illustrating Topics	People Related to Topic
Story 1: Mr. Murgatroyd, President Grover Cleveland's ambassador to Antarctica, who later became known as "the Skinflint Industrialist"	1. The portrait of Mr. Murgatroyd done when he was ambassador 2. The table that belonged to Mr. Murgatroyd 3. The chair that Mr. Murgatroyd used in his ice hut in Antarctica	1. Mr. Murgatroyd 2. Mrs. Murgatroyd, who traveled with Mr. Murgatroyd to Antarctica, became an explorer, and was the first woman to reach the South Pole 3. Daughter Murgatroyd, the first American born in Antarctica
Story 2: Hannah, who saved the house from being burned by rioters in 1911	1. Charred floorboards 2. Brick thrown through the window	1. Hannah 2. Joseph Garsini, the brick-throwing radical
Story 3: A tertiary story	1. Object 1 2. Object 2 3. Object 3 [Note that the number of objects may vary.]	1. Person 1 2. Person 2 3. Person 3

Context
Background information that may help visitors to understand better what they are seeing in this space, such as the following:

1. *Broad piece of information 1:* This might be general information about Antarctica, perhaps touching on themes of exploration, adventure, and discovery.

(*continued*)

2. *Broad piece of background information 2:* This might be background about the 1911 riot in response to Mr. Murgatroyd's cutting the wages of his factory workers, many of whom were recent Italian immigrants to America. This could prompt discussion related to immigration, class, civil unrest, or violence, all issues with wide-ranging potential resonance for visitors.

Textbox 1.4 is one of a number contained in a document. Together, these forms describe spaces at the Garsini House and structure the interpretation as a whole. This space-by-space approach highlights the key objects and stories to be covered in each part of the museum, inside and outside. It links stories that people can understand with objects they can see and experience, while at the same time touching on bigger, broader human experiences to which all visitors can likely relate. Though particularly useful for tour guides, these forms have endured as an effective tool for training all visitor service staff.

Interpretive planning documents should focus on the best song but be broad enough to address multiple ways of delivering it. Some people like to go to a live concert, others to sing in the shower, listen to their iPods, or hum along to the car radio. A good interpretive plan allows for—indeed, encourages—the presentation of interpretive themes in a number of formats. A guided tour, an exhibition, a publication, a program or special event—all are simply different forms of conveying information. No matter which form is adopted, and several forms will almost certainly be employed, all should have at their core some or all of the interpretive messages developed and described in your interpretive plan.

How Do We Train the Chorus?
Training for Frontline Staff

Once the songs are decided and the music has been distributed, it is time to train and practice. Rehearsal should include everyone. Although there will be a few lead singers, the chorus, other musicians, stage crew, and all others have a responsibility to know and understand the music on some level and what performance will take place on that day.

Virtually every museum has a Margaret, a star guide who is amusing, engaging, and entertaining in equal measure. She knows all there is to know and can spin factually accurate yarns for hours, entertaining even the most bored

TEXTBOX 1.5

CASE STUDY: BALANCING CREATIVE INTERPRETATION AND PROGRAMMING

The Wychwood Museum is located in an underserved area with a high crime rate. Since its foundation in 1972, its professional staff has conceived of it as a traditional historic house museum, offering guided tours and revealing the life of one family over three hundred years (how familiar does that sound?). Its three-acre site was once a farm, and even though it is in an urban area, its green space and famous peony gardens were well known and highly valued by community members and regional plant enthusiasts. Nevertheless, it stood behind a high wooden fence and was only open to the public a limited number of hours per week.

Acting on feedback from the local community, the Wychwood Museum developed the idea to hold a farmer's market, very much in line with its interpretive focus. Some of the produce was grown on the museum site, with local farmers providing the rest. The market, which took place on the street outside, raised a number of issues. Although it was an innovative, community-based program, the market took place on Friday evenings in the summer, outside the normal operating hours of the museum, but at a time when people actually wanted to buy produce for the weekend. The site wrestled with how to ensure safety and keep the site open "out of hours." Would the museum be open? Would people really want to take tours before or after buying their turnips and tomatoes?

Reorganizing staffing and volunteer arrangements, the Wychwood Museum was able to make it happen. The market ran every week from May to September, drawing a whole new audience. Many of these shoppers took the time to explore this interesting place where they had never been. Some came back repeatedly, often bringing family or friends. The staff and volunteers agreed to give up part of their Friday evenings to allow this to happen, employing their interpretation in a brief, pithy way that suited the time, event, and audience. The Wychwood Museum Farmer's Market sent a welcome signal that the museum was eager to meet the community's needs rather than ask the community to meet its needs.

adult or rambunctious child. We can all aspire to be Margarets, but it is all right if we are not. Remember, you do not need to know everything. Few do, and many extremely capable guides give excellent tours with a good structure and basic information.

Good guiding requires a willingness to listen to and to converse with your visitors. A good guide should be the agent who invites visitors to interact with what they are seeing and experiencing, who offers enough information to get the audience thinking and interacting with the space and objects around them so that they become participants in the creation of their experience.

Guides especially should be trained in content and communication. Their job is to make the site friendly, welcoming, and accessible, not to trap visitors there longer than they want to be, imparting all that is known about the site and the collection. Not only do they need to know the relevant material, but they must be aware of how to convey it in a way that is accessible and sensitive to their audience.

Issue written material to help guides learn about the museum. Guide training materials might include

- copies of the interpretive plan;
- information about good guiding skills;
- relevant articles related to your museum;
- a bibliography of useful sources.

All of these important tools are essential for equipping a guide (and others) with the necessary background knowledge to be effective.

Interpreters can invite participation by introducing ideas in one space that guests can then observe for themselves in another. Many museums can be viewed as a kind of archeological object that has survived through time. At a historic house, for instance, we may know a lot about the people and things that were there in the eighteenth century; in many cases, actual objects in the collection may be original to the house. Where we lack knowledge, there are holes. A strategy that can work well is to engage visitors by inviting them to think as cocurators, imparting what we do know but encouraging them to think about the mysteries that remain in terms of our knowledge about the museum and its collection.

Other practices can help in training. Create a learning environment in your museum by encouraging guides and staff to learn from each other and from visitors. One training strategy is to assign a guide in training to study a space and then give a tour of it to other guides and staff. This can seem intimidating, but it is just practice. Another effective approach is to have guides in training hold a trainee status for a period while they shadow, or follow, various guides to study other strategies. Guides might discuss their style, knowledge, and approach with fellow guides, staff, and volunteers. They can follow someone else's tour, picking up pointers about content and presentation.[5]

It is important to add that while there might be a star singer in every band, the backup vocalists count a great deal as well. Every person responsible for the operation of the museum should be trained to a basic level about interpretation. Whether answering the office phone, selling a ticket, or directing a visitor to the bathroom, anyone is liable to be asked a question about the museum, what it is, and what it stands for. Board members must be knowledgeable, too, for those business-meeting moments and cocktail party chitchats. Make staff and volunteers aware of other cultural institutions and activities in the area and, importantly, how your museum relates to them. Encourage them to visit and offer team-building field trips to these sites for guides, staff, and board members. The better prepared they are to answer such questions, the better the perception of your museum.

Following from this, make sure to demand a positive, knowledgeable, friendly demeanor of everyone who comes into contact with the public in any way. Many a positive visitor experience can be attributed not to the collection or

Photo 1.2. Paid and volunteer staff at all levels of your small museum will come into contact with visitors and must be able to be good public relations officers, offering helpful information about the site. (Courtesy of Historic Germantown, Philadelphia, Pennsylvania)

TEXTBOX 1.6

EXAMPLE: MAXINE THE HOUSEKEEPER

Maxine was an institution. She had worked part-time at the Francis Art Museum for years, cleaning collections and offering a hand with various programs and events. Her work was so good that three or four smaller area museums asked if she could spend a little time every couple of weeks doing their cleaning. Although she had never given a formal tour in her life, Maxine was always in evidence. Whether wandering from building to building or dodging school tours as she tried to do some tidying, she was always around. She was a friendly face, and occasionally, when she came into a gallery as a tour was leaving, a visitor would ask her a question. She always tried to answer honestly and graciously.

Maxine had probably dispensed more information to a wider range of people than most tour guides. For many visitors, she was one of the most important public faces of the institution, often the first person they encountered, the one who first told them "when this place was built," directed them to the bathrooms, or pointed out where to get tickets. She had given background information about the history and collections over and over and had a remarkable capacity to connect dots, having worked in several nearby museums. Officially, her job title was housekeeper, but her role as an interpreter could not be overstated. Few people were more important as an example of the pervasiveness of good interpretive practice.

guided tour but to the helpfulness with which a staff person assists with directions or patiently responds to a special need.

The keys to effective interpretation are to be a good listener, to know your information, and to offer it as needed, being sensitive to visitors, their interests, and their time. Another key to guiding is practice. Like living, guiding reflects experience built over time. The better you understand your music, and the more you practice, the better you will become! And remember, at your museum, interpretation should be part of everyone's job description. If you work with the chorus, you are a potential performer.

Performance Time! Implementation of Interpretation

Performance can take many different forms. The key here is that you recognize that good interpretation—the themes you have worked hard to develop—should be a component of every performance, from start to finish. As this chapter has stressed, the guided tour is one choice for delivering interpretation, but there are many others. Some of these are covered in other parts of the book, particularly exhibitions and programs.

The premise of a famous 1970s television show was a three-hour tour that turned into a disaster. None of us want our museums to be a bad sitcom or compared to one. Hence, the three-hour tour—*do not do it.* The same goes for the two- and even the one-hour tour. Do not do them either. Make your standard tours snappy and relatively brief. Emphasize the main points that have been clearly laid out in your interpretive plan. At the same time, maintain flexibility to adjust to the situation.

Flexibility is crucial to audience-centered interpretation. A good interpretive plan should offer multiple options and vehicles for the visitor and the tour guide alike. Not every visitor will respond in the same way. Engage your visitors, getting to know about their interests and why they are there. Tour guides and other frontline service staff can ask simple questions to gauge level of interest and knowledge. Local visitors to institutions in Philadelphia may know more about Quakers and William Penn than those from Boston, Butte, or Bangladesh. Try not to assume any knowledge but gain a sense for the visitor so that the most effective presentation can be constructed.

You will know in those uncommon instances when Mr. and Mrs. Supercollector come through the door and want to hear all about every painting, stick of furniture, and piece of pewter. We can prepare for these rare occurrences but not plan for them. Become attuned to when these folks arrive. If it happens to you and you do not know your trifid foot from a teapot or your Caravaggio from your Klimt, not to worry. Tours can and should be experiential on both sides and Mr. and Mrs. Supercollector probably have a great deal of information to impart.

Engage in conversation. Learn from them. Although extensive knowledge can easily seem intimidating, be honest about your own strengths. Chances are you know more about your museum and its collection than even the most knowledgeable visitor. At the same time, on-the-job training can be welcome, and nothing can be more thrilling than a tour where you take away as much as—or more than—the person paying to be there. If you are engaged and interested, chances are that Mr. and Mrs. Supercollector will go away delighted to have found a like-minded person, flattered that they have been able to share their expertise, and impressed with the museum.

This can be tricky if the hungry family of four is on the same tour and trying to zip through the museum in an effort to see everything before lunch. This situation requires special attention, and training and practice pay off here. If you have a clear idea of the important themes you are trying to convey, are familiar with your collections, and have practiced, you should be able to structure an excellent brief tour, incorporating a great deal of good information into their experience. Being flexible, you can then invite Mr. and Mrs. Supercollector to return with you to look at special objects.

Or, in another scenario, your well-conceived and forward-thinking interpretive plan may have been used to develop both guided and self-guided tours. In this instance, the hungry family of four might be given your museum's "Family Fun Go-by-Yourself Scavenger Hunt Tour," while Mr. and Mrs. Supercollector receive a more detailed experience in keeping with their interests. Naturally, these episodes present challenges that every museum—and guide—faces, and how you handle them will be the measure of your institution.

TEXTBOX 1.7

PROBLEMS AND THE IMPORTANCE OF THE GUIDE

There are always problems, and tour guides need to be ready for many eventualities. At Oaktree, a historic site, a guide was driven to the limit of patience on one tour by a family with a small, unhappy infant. The museum had a trade-off policy: Parents with children were gently encouraged to let one parent take a tour while the other wandered the grounds and gardens before they traded off. The parents in this case wanted none of that, insisting that they and their little cherub should take the tour together. Disruption followed. People became unhappy with the infant's crying, which made the tour difficult to hear. When moving from one room to the next, the tour guide quipped, "You can just follow the screaming baby," which drew laughter from some of the tour but annoyed and embarrassed the parents, who promptly left. Mission accomplished—or was it?

While possibly amusing and perhaps even somewhat understandable, this sort of comment is the antithesis of good interpretation. A difficult situation was made worse and could have been handled in a more professional manner. The guide might have quickly asked a colleague to spend a few minutes giving the parents and their child a private tour to prevent their impinging on others' enjoyment. He could have quietly asked the parents to wait for the next guide, noting that although he certainly appreciated that they wanted to have a tour, he needed to ensure that all visitors had equal opportunity to partake of a good experience.

Snap judgments are often part of the tour guide's job, and it is important to remember at all times that conduct must be measured, friendly, enthusiastic, and open. Surveys at similar museums to Oaktree have borne out that some of the most important criteria for whether visitors have a good experience include the behavior, professionalism, and skill of the guide.

What Do the Critics Say and How Do We Do Better? Evaluation and Revision

A critical component of good interpretive practice is evaluation. You want to know what people think, and you should not be scared of the result. Although evaluation can sometimes feel like an afterthought or one additional thing to do, it must be taken seriously. At the end of a tour or an exciting program, you may want simply to sit down and have a rest or to clean up the tables and chairs and go home. But you need to make the effort to see what people think of what you did. Even though visitors often want to get away after a tour or event, find a way to make it easy for them to offer feedback.

The best institutions evaluate virtually everything they do. Make it clear to visitors at the outset of their experience that you will be asking them for feedback. Then, end your tour five minutes early and tell them that you really want to know what they think. Suggest they are really helping the museum by offering their opinions. Some of the same methods used in the initial stages of interpretive development, such as interviews or focus groups, can also yield good results. The AASLH and the American Association of Museums have regular programs that can help with evaluation, bringing in consultants or structuring a formal survey that is then analyzed in depth. Building your interpretation on the results of previous audience feedback will send an important message that you are interested in visitors' views and will act on them.

Find multiple ways for visitors to give feedback. Visitors can be asked to fill out surveys or remarks cards. Have a comment box. Perhaps an old computer could be set up to allow visitors to do a two-minute online survey. Naturally, capturing evaluations when people are at your museum is by far the most effective way, but you can also offer a feedback form on your website. If you have collected names, addresses, and e-mails, you can do a targeted mailing. Send a link to a Web survey. Again, do not forget how technology can be used to help.

The best interpretive process is active, and revision should occur. In other words, while adhering to your core set of themes and concepts, respond to feedback by making changes as necessary. That does not mean you respond to every comment you receive in the visitor box. But as you review multiple sources of information gleaned from evaluations, if specific comments begin to recur, it is time to consider revision. If you get one bad review from a cranky critic, you can probably ignore it. If you are tackling a difficult subject and elicit a lot of emotional response, this is not necessarily bad (and most often is good). If you are touching people on a deep level, you are probably doing pretty well. But in the event of a slew of bad reviews, you need to make some changes. Relying on the ideas of people who have been interested enough to visit your museum and offer feedback is an ideal place to start.

Do not let excuses rather than reasons interfere with changing interpretation. If the answer to a criticism is, "But that is the way we have always sung that piece," then this is an excuse. If, on the other hand, the criticism asks your mariachi band to sing opera, there may be a good reason you do not, and never will, take it into account. In handling feedback about interpretation, know the difference. But you fail to revise, on the basis of good evaluations, to your museum's peril.

Most likely, feedback will be generally positive. If you have gone through all the steps outlined in this chapter, there is an excellent chance that you will have garnered feedback beforehand, and there should be few surprises. Your interpretation will be well planned, based on good information from a range of sources and people, supported by solid documentation, and well executed by trained personnel.

In playing a vibrant role in public service, though, small museums cannot rest on their laurels. Plan to change things as often as practicable. Tell a new story within your interpretive framework, introduce a new artifact, give a different type of tour, or offer a new program or exhibit frequently. Small institutions often have limited resources, but doing this sort of thing need not take a great deal of time, money, or effort. If the innovation is planned well beforehand and fits seamlessly within the broader interpretive framework set by your institution, it will be much easier to achieve.

Although we all have a favorite type of music, and probably a favorite tune that we like to hear over and over again, nothing can be more thrilling than the sound of a new arrangement, or hearing an old favorite played in a different way.

Conclusion

Good interpretation should make your museum more accessible. When clear, coherent messages are transmitted to visitors throughout their experience of your museum, they will understand and want to keep coming back to understand and experience more. Offer a range of programming geared to meet the needs of various audiences according to their age, interest, learning style, and other criteria. In the museum world, one size does not fit all. Visitors want structure, but they also want choice. Successful interpretive planning will create a framework that will underpin all that you do in presenting your museum to the public.

This chapter has discussed the importance of placing interpretation, broadly defined, at the center of your museum's activities. To provide this public service, you need to think carefully ahead of time about what is important about your museum. To help with this thinking, you need to recruit other people with good ideas to offer advice and guidance. You should work hard to understand your audience and their interests. Then you are ready to put ideas

CASE STUDY: TOUR PLANNING, DEVELOPMENT, AND EVALUATION

Fact Finders was a new school tour, bringing several thousand schoolchildren to a museum that had limited numbers before. It was one outgrowth of an interpretive plan for the museum. Although this was a positive development, it caused some consternation. The guides were not sure how to relate to children. The curator envisaged wear and tear on the building and collections. The board had nightmares about a lot of sticky fingers touching objects or, worse, theft. All of these concerns had to be factored into planning the tour program, allowing the many schoolchildren to feel unencumbered at the museum while balancing preservation needs.

In the start-up phase, a curriculum was developed that closely adhered to local and state school standards. A pilot year of a small number of classes helped to work out the bugs in the program. Museum staff and volunteers worked with teachers to determine what might work and what would not. Activities were developed with an eye toward making the program fun and educational. Students were kept moving and given a range of things to do. Guides were specially recruited for the Fact Finders tours and provided with training not only in the museum's interpretation but also in the special Fact Finders interpretation. Finally, there was extensive evaluation of the program, with questions about everything from scheduling and transportation to the Fact Finders website, to the Barn Scavenger Hunt component. This led to changes—some substantial, some just minor tweaks—every year.

Seven years later, Fact Finders was still running. It had won national awards for excellence and introduced over ten thousand schoolchildren to the museum and local historic resources. A corps of well-trained specialist guides had developed; their expertise came in handy for other programs beyond Fact Finders. Although all those school visits raised some conservation issues, they were much less serious than feared. Working within the institution's interpretive plan, Fact Finders represented a huge leap in providing public service and welcoming a new audience. Visions of schoolchildren running wild had been deftly dealt with through comprehensive planning, a concise structure, engaging interpretation, special training, and rigorous evaluation.

on paper, summing up your themes and developing a written plan that links museum-specific content to larger ideas and experiences.

Once all that is in place, you can train guides and other frontline personnel, be they staff or volunteers, to convey your themes with confidence, accuracy, and enthusiasm. They should practice repeatedly and understand the importance to the institution of doing this well. No matter what form the interpretation takes—tours, exhibits, programs, events—it should be evaluated, with necessary revisions incorporated. Defining the "song you sing best" will pay handsome dividends, and you and your institution will be more than ready to put on concert after successful concert.

Resources

The following annotated bibliography of selected works might be especially helpful in interpretation and guide training.

Diamond, Judy, Jessica J. Luke, and David H. Uttal. *Practical Evaluation Guide: Tools for Museums and Other Informal Educational Settings.* Lanham, MD: AltaMira Press, 2009. This straightforward guide includes chapters with sample questions for conducting interviews as well as designing and administering questionnaires and demographic surveys. The book also explains options for presenting and analyzing data and offers sound advice for putting results into practice and helping your organization develop an evaluative institutional culture.

Donnelly, Jessica Foy, ed. *Interpreting Historic House Museums.* Walnut Creek, CA: AltaMira Press, 2002. This edited volume of essays covers all aspects of historic site interpretation from planning to encompassing the history of the whole site and all the diverse peoples who have lived and worked there, to house presentation and furnishings, to guide training and Americans with Disabilities Act accessibility, to programs and experiential learning.

Grinder, Alison L., and E. Sue McCoy. *The Good Guide: A Sourcebook for Interpreters, Docents, and Tour Guides.* Scottsdale, AZ: Ironwood Press, 1989. This is the classic work on how to behave—and how not to behave—as a museum docent.

Levy, Barbara Abramoff. "Interpretation Planning: Why and How." In *Interpreting Historic House Museums,* edited by Jessica Foy Donnelly, 43–60. Walnut Creek, CA: AltaMira Press, 2002. This concise essay is an excellent overview of an interpretive planning and implementation process and a good place to start. It sums up the purpose a plan fills in the organizational mission and offers a good overview of the process that is somewhat more approachable than *Great Tours!* (see next entry).

Levy, Barbara Abramoff, Sandra Mackenzie Lloyd, and Susan Porter Schreiber. *Great Tours! Thematic Tours and Guide Training for Historic Sites.* Walnut Creek, CA: AltaMira Press, 2002. *Great Tours!* lays out the steps for developing excellent guided tours from start to finish—encompassing everything from how much staff time to expect to dedicate to the project of developing great tours to guide training. The book is filled with pages of work sheets that can be easily reproduced and distributed to your staff and team to complete the exercises.

Serrell, Beverly. *Exhibit Labels: An Interpretive Approach*. Walnut Creek, CA: AltaMira Press, 1996. Although largely about writing effective exhibit labels, this book is an excellent how-to guide. Serrell believes that good labels begin with good interpretive communication; therefore, she covers many of the core principles of interpretation in the introductory chapters.

Stenton. "The Interpretive Plan." http://stenton.org/index.php/history-collections-and -interpretation/the-interprative-plan (accessed May 3, 2011). The website for the historic house museum at which the authors developed many of the ideas in this chapter has a copy of the interpretive plan created for that site in 2003.

Tilden, Freeman. *Interpreting Our Heritage*. Chapel Hill: University of North Carolina Press, 1957, 1977, 1997, 2008. This museum classic includes Tilden's six principles of interpretation, which, despite his 1950s use of language, continue to serve as the foundation for much thinking in the field about interpretation.

Notes

1. The authors would like to thank Anne L. B. Burnett for her insights vis-à-vis this chapter. Many outstanding and valued colleagues have helped to shape our thinking about the subject over time, especially David W. Young, Sandy Lloyd, Barbara Silberman, Bernard L. Herman, Candace Tangorra Matelic, Page Talbott, and Rosalind Remer.

2. See Freeman Tilden, *Interpreting Our Heritage* (Chapel Hill: University of North Carolina Press, 1957, 1977, 1997, 2008).

3. The AASLH program, called Visitors Count!, can be found at www.aaslh.org/visitorscount. The Institute of Museums and Library Service and the American Association of Museums offer the Museum Assessment Program (MAP), which has a Public Dimension Assessment (PDA). See www.aam-us.org/museumresources/map.

4. For a sample budget worksheet, see Barbara Abramoff Levy, Sandra Mackenzie Lloyd, and Susan Porter Schreiber, *Great Tours! Thematic Tours and Guide Training for Historic Sites* (Walnut Creek, CA: AltaMira Press, 2001), 15.

5. See, especially, Meggett B. Lavin, "Building a Tool Kit for Your Interpreters: Methods of Success from Drayton Hall," in *Interpreting Historic House Museums*, ed. Jessica Foy Donnelly (Walnut Creek, CA: AltaMira Press, 2002), 251–68. This chapter details the how-tos of building a well-trained, invested, self-perpetuating, professional guide corps and a positive culture of learning that pervades your museum.

INTERPRETING DIFFICULT ISSUES
Madeline C. Flagler

D ifficult, challenging, uncomfortable, necessary—these words describe
interpretation issues being explored at most historic sites and museums
throughout the country. Issues related to class structure, immigration,
slavery, Native Americans, native Hawaiians, African Americans, and women
are all vital components of American history and present multilevel challenges
to volunteers, staff, and boards of directors at each site. History is often seen as
inert, restricted to facts and dates. In reality, history is vibrant. Barbara Tuchman says that history is "like a design seen through a kaleidoscope": "When the
cylinder is shaken, the countless colored fragments form a new picture."[1] As you
examine history from different points of view, it resembles a changing landscape,
and when the issues are sensitive or difficult, change meets a natural resistance.
Successful interpretation requires cultivation of your museum board and staff,
your frontline interpreters, and your audience and community. This will demand
patience, persistence, and listening. With a commitment to the goal of expanded
interpretation and using fundamental guidelines for best practices, even a small
museum with limited staff can create and implement an interpretive plan that
addresses difficult issues in a way that the American Association for State and
Local History (AASLH) Standards and Excellence Program for History Organizations (StEPs) describes as ethical, effective, and inclusive and that museums
find inherently rewarding.

The payoffs are far-reaching. The institution's sustainability is strengthened
by more inclusive interpretive programs, but there are consequences that are
more widespread and perhaps of greater value. The dynamic and fulfilling results of newly researched and thoughtfully constructed interpretive programs are
the rewards for the energy and dedication it takes for implementation. Benefits
include the sense of furthering local discourse, inclusion of the historically disenfranchised, and broadening the perspectives of the general audience. Reaching
out to those who are not included in the traditional narrative ties us more closely
to our communities. Finding a way to expose all our audiences to new ideas and
new perspectives creates energy by engaging instead of lecturing.

My primary museum experience has been as education director at two sites where difficult or sensitive social, political, and cultural issues were addressed as major components of the interpretation. Both sites began as museums featuring the stories of prominent white families. Including the narratives of native Hawaiians at Mission Houses Museum in Honolulu, Hawaii, has been an ongoing process for about thirty years. More inclusive interpretation of the enslaved men, women, and children at the Bellamy Mansion in Wilmington, North Carolina, is far more recent. Once the home of a local plantation owner, the Bellamy Mansion Museum, located in an urban site, is distinguished by an intact slave quarters and an architecturally significant main house. Mission Houses Museum has three historic buildings, one of which was brought in pieces from Boston with the first company of missionaries arriving in Honolulu in 1820. This first-hand experience at sites where there were deep challenges and exciting rewards has been enlightening on many levels.

Change Happens

A generation or two ago, it was common practice to keep the interiors of house museums behind Plexiglas. Cases and wall panels were used extensively for museum exhibits. Set tours were recited verbatim by guides. As museums and staff evolved and museum studies programs became widespread, a reexamination of common interpretive practices led the museum community to see these as impediments to the full museum experience. How could the audience experience be best facilitated? Changes were made; Plexiglas was limited; use of wall exhibits and display cases was scaled back. As visitors were allowed more physical access to rooms, other barriers were questioned. Set tours were modified in favor of more interactive and individualized unscripted tours, though with continued stress on accuracy and authenticity. Wider access to buildings revealed a need to interpret the working zones as well as the family and formal zones. Interpretation continued to evolve and became more inclusive, tackling intellectual as well as emotional barriers, as it had earlier approached physical ones. Change was in the air. Suddenly museum interpretation was in difficult waters.

As museums work to broaden their narratives from traditional commemorations, they move into areas that require a delicate balance to present a true and authentic story without stereotypes and prejudgments. There are several components to accomplishing a successful, inclusive narrative presented by a small museum. In some ways, the simple fact that the museum is small places limitations on interpretation. Smaller spaces require smaller exhibits, which can thus include fewer words, so that images and phrasing need to be carefully chosen. A smaller staff faces increased demands; thus, research and training may take longer to complete.

TEXTBOX 2.1

JONKONNU

Jonkonnu is a traditional, pre–Civil War, African American celebration. The Bellamy Mansion Museum, an antebellum historic house museum in Wilmington, North Carolina, decided to reenact this event. There was strong but not voluminous documentation. The museum wanted to highlight the fact that, given a small window of time between Christmas and New Year's, the local enslaved population took the opportunity to re-create features of their African roots. From all accounts, it was a time of festivity. From the rare documentation by former slaves, it was a time of careful planning with the most significant activities occurring in the slave quarters, away from the white population. Drumming, call-and-response songs, dance, and storytelling were components of Jonkonnu.

The museum began with a set of goals for the interpretation that emphasized the agency of those who prevailed in honoring their heritage from within a system that actively denied them their past. Organizers contacted a group in New Bern, North Carolina, that had been reenacting Jonkonnu for several years. They were helpful in relating the public reaction they had encountered across the state. There was concern that the Bellamy Jonkonnu needed to be sensitive to the undignified and cartoonish portrayals of African American culture during the times of slavery. The museum researched Jonkonnu across eastern North Carolina to gather as much information as possible. Board members became involved, and organizers made contacts with leaders in the African American community. The event would be held at the historic site but the museum wanted to involve as much of the community as possible, so organizers saw that contacting performance artists was a natural next step.

The museum developed an interpretive piece that involved speaking roles incorporated with dancers, drummers, two local pastors, griots (storytellers), and other artists and leaders to create an event set in the times of slavery but able to celebrate respectfully the tenacity and creativity with which enslaved men, women, and children held on to their preslavery roots. There was a record turnout for the day with enthusiastic audience participation and great media coverage. Currently, Jonkonnu is an annual event, with the Bellamy Mansion Museum exploring ways to include the broader community more widely.

Photo 2.1. Jonkonnu at Bellamy Mansion Museum Slave Quarters, December 2008. (Courtesy of Ann Hertzler)

Community input is essential both to a balanced perspective and to local, broad-based community buy-in to an enhanced but difficult interpretive program. The challenges of interpreting difficult issues are rewarded by the fact that the museum's volunteer base, attendance, membership, and funders can all grow as a result of appealing to the wider community. Expanding interpretation widens your audience, broadens community entities that find value in your organization, connects you to national conversations on historical issues, and increases long-term sustainability. Sustainability is strengthened through wider membership appeal and repeat visits.[2] New interpretation of difficult issues allows sites to connect to others undergoing similar changes, providing an additional support network.[3] Change creates a fresh feel and exciting dynamic that can spread from the board and staff to the audience and community. The sustainability problems faced by house museums have been closely examined in recent years,[4] but a vital, dynamic site that has a broad base of community stakeholders is better prepared to survive this trend in any economic climate.

Issues of inclusion at historic sites have been gradually gaining ground from as early as the late 1980s. When Jennifer Eichstedt and Stephen Small began their surveys in 1996 for their book *Representations of Slavery: Race and Ideology in Southern Plantation Museums,*[5] the interpretive landscape was beginning to change even in some of the conservative areas they examined. By the book's 2002 publication, many of the changes they advocated were already in process. *Representations of Slavery* is helpful in understanding the limitations, pitfalls, and distortions of not using an examined, scholarly approach and considering only a thin layer of the social fabric. An old, worn-out story is ultimately told, creating a dry, static experience offensive to modern sensibilities and dull in its scope. This experience does nothing to encourage repeat visits by a broad-based audience, does not contribute to the general discourse, and fails to inspire donors.

In her 2006 dissertation, "Rethinking Representations of Slave Life at Historical Plantation Museums: Towards a Commemorative Museum Pedagogy,"[6] Julia Rose addresses the change of interpretation at a plantation site from a Euro-American-centered tour to one that includes the enslaved people who lived and worked there. She describes a goal of ethical, multidimensional interpretation. She posits that the enslaved African Americans should be honestly and authentically represented and their full humanity within the context of slavery addressed.

Rose sees interpretation of slave life at many plantation sites as flat. Many of the slaves in the narrative have neither names nor occupations. Filial relationships are not explored. The house tour is preoccupied with the white family and its opulent lifestyle. Elaborate decorative arts are important features of the tour, but the enslaved people who outnumbered the white family many times over are anonymous and inconsequential. A fair or ethical interpretation of the site fully includes the enslaved population with multidimensional narratives of who they were.[7] These criteria are clearly in line with educational and interpretation standards adopted by the AASLH and the American Association of Museums (AAM).

Issues of discrimination, lack of civil rights, and slavery are often new territory and require long-term effort to succeed with the public and staff. Over the past twenty years, scholars and respected institutions have established the issues being addressed as important to an honest national narrative, but this is still making its way into public consciousness. We see ourselves as a nation born to counter injustices in Europe. Our self-image does not include slavery, human trafficking, prejudice, denial of civil rights, violence, and the inhumanity of man to man. Our country was established as a refuge from the social and political evils of the world. American democracy is still presented as the answer to regimes that deny human rights and equality. American slavery, gender and racial injustices, and their long-running aftermath run counter to this narrative. It is hard to find the positive in this story, and it is uncomfortable for all participants. But for the same reason that it is important to address the painful history of the Holocaust, it is important to address the facts of injustice in this country. And just as there is celebration of the stalwart survival and fortitude of the oppressed and persecuted Jews and those who saved and aided them, Americans have the opportunity to create a similar context. Within the constraints of a system that denied the humanity of a race, there are truths of incredible fortitude and agency. These stories give the history of slavery in this country a face. Stories of individuals and groups who built valuable and contributing lives for themselves and others and displayed courage and mental and emotional strength in spite of oppression are a part of this difficult history.

As you develop your interpretation, finding a balance between the reality of the inhumanity of the system and the very human drive to prevail takes time. Again, use of the standards and tapping into scholarly discourse and research will greatly aid in this endeavor and in answering questions from the public. Input from community leaders and educators will give additional perspective to the process. Here, connecting to the community can be deeply rewarding. There are narratives in the special collections of your local library, in locally published books, and in the hands of church historians and community groups. As your network widens, you will find that the stewards of these histories welcome partnerships to honor their communities.

Addressing the Public

Sites are finding that their relationship with the audience on these issues is undergoing a transition. Some sites have discovered that their audience is unfamiliar with the concepts of broader interpretation; others are finding that their audience is already aware of information that the site considers new.[8] A narrative that is new to visitors, running counter to their understanding of the subject and reaching beyond their comfort level, can spur them to question both the facts and the perspective of the institution. A well-informed docent can invite audience members to take the same journey they themselves have experienced, where examination of primary documents and readings of broad history have informed a new context. On the other hand, when the audience is familiar with the subject of a broader interpretation, a less-informed docent can be put on the defensive. Docents who are ready for and comfortable with questions can provide the best of interactive museum experiences. No computer screen can compare to two real people asking real questions of one another in honest discourse within a real historical landscape.

An example of addressing questions from a tour as an opportunity for real exchange comes from tours given at the Bellamy Mansion Museum's urban slave quarters. The museum site includes a two-story, brick, Italianate slave quarters fifty feet from the mansion's back door. We have often heard the public comment on how nice this building is. Indeed, its design is clearly in keeping with the refined Italianate architecture of the big house, and it is much better constructed than slave quarters on most plantations. Its upper windows are delicately arched, and even in the midst of being restored, the quarters have a solid feel. This "nice" comment provides an opportunity to draw the audience members out of their comfort zone of expected reality and help them step into the shoes of those who lived in this space. Docents are able to have visitors step away from the building into the yard. They can point out how the quarters are situated on the lot—in the corner on the back property line. There are no windows in the back wall, just as there are none in the back wall of the carriage house, the other structure built on the property line. The windows to the west looked out on the chicken house and the carriage house and stables, giving limited visibility and ventilation and close proximity to noxious fumes from the animals. The quarters were typical of urban sites in that the sleeping areas were in the same building as the workspaces. These quarters have a laundry, where the work required heat and humidity in a climate that is often hot and humid enough, and a "necessary," or an indoor privy, with its associated odors. Yes, there is a solid elegance to the structure, but its realities were not those of comfort and convenience. And yes, the life of an enslaved house servant in an urban center was far different from, and much more comfortable than, that of an enslaved field hand. Yet, to quote Richard Starobin commenting on the phenomenon of urban slavery, "[It] might be supposed not to be so hard as one would imagine. . . . But slavery is slavery wherever it is found."[9]

Tools for Interpreting Difficult Issues

Standards are set up to facilitate the process and promote professionalism. With difficult issues not always understood by the public or your board, careful use of a framework based on standards can be invaluable as you move from concept to creation to implementation—from *why* to *how* to *when* to *how can we do it better*. Interpretation of difficult issues will require special attention to cultivation, mission statements, community input, teamwork, leadership, and continuing reexamination and refinement.

Standards for interpretation from both the AASLH and AAM demand clear, quality context based on scholarly primary research. Interpretation is education based, aided by community feedback and regular staff training. Regular assessments to plan and improve interpretative activities can be accomplished through periodic, scheduled surveys of staff and visitors and through community advisors. As described by the AASLH standards, the interpretation process is fluid and dynamic, not set or static. The goal is a balance between scholarly research that connects the museum to the national dialogue concerning our history and community input that connects the museum to the needs, concerns, and issues that relate to the community the museum serves. Because the issues involved are complex and nuanced, having a framework of standards will aid you when you encounter difficulties at each step—statement of purpose, research, narrative, and implementation.

Interpretive Statement of Purpose

An interpretive statement of purpose with clear ties to the institution's mission will aid in navigating themes and addressing audiences in interpretive programs. This is particularly effective as you negotiate a new, more difficult interpretation. Both AAM and AASLH standards stress the importance of "clearly stating [your] overall educational goals, philosophy, and messages."[10] By beginning with a statement of purpose for your interpretation, you have a reference point as you determine what kind of research needs to be done and where to look for it, as you are planning interpretation content and techniques and, perhaps most importantly, as you relate your message to the public.

An interpretive statement of purpose is also important as you cultivate understanding and support of your interpretation. It will help in communications with the media and community. With a statement of purpose, you can clearly make your case to the board and guides. With addressing difficult issues and the ensuing interpretation that has not been a part of the site's traditional narrative, there is a common institutional fear of changing course into areas that may distort the museum's identity and message. Using the museum's mission statement to develop a statement of purpose for the expanded interpretation can address these fears. It gives a solid base from which to work and can set clear goals for tours and programming. A clear statement of goals and message aids you as you make your case for the interpretation's importance in increasing sustainability and community stakeholding and broadening your audience. As new African American programming was developed at the Bellamy Mansion Museum, a clear, focused interpretation statement of purpose was created and used in board reports, brochures, and press releases.[11] It was particularly helpful when dealing with the media to clarify the fine points of promoting advocacy within the programs on sensitive issues.

Research: Difficulty Can Be Opportunity

A common explanation when a site is asked about its limited or absent interpretation of historically disenfranchised groups, be they African American, Native American, native Hawaiian, or women, is a lack of adequate research. "We want to, but there just is no information." In Susan Schreiber's "Interpreting Slavery at National Trust Sites: A Case Study in Addressing Difficult Topics,"[12] trust sites considering more inclusion of slavery in their tours cited concern as to whether there was "enough research . . . for substantive interpretation." The frustration of finding little information after diligently looking for primary sources in all the logical and well-traveled repositories is understandable. It is difficult. Interpretive standards of best practices reiterate the best instincts of a historian and educator only to give information to the public that has been well researched and documented. It is difficult logistically, and it is difficult when the subject is complex, multilayered, and subtle. Even when you have the best basic information, converting it into a judicious, authentic, and authoritative interpretation digestible by the public is a challenge.

Often sites are concerned that new interpretation on a new subject means they will be tossing out previous research and losing the interpretations that they have been honing for years. Authentic scholarly research is not lost but becomes a part of the greater picture. The history of the American Revolution cannot be told without the stories of George Washington, Benjamin Franklin, and James Madison, but to tell only those stories would give a very one-dimensional picture. To tell their stories without the difficult information that each of these three great men owned slaves—and two of them owned a substantial number—would not be giving as true a picture as we can. The fact that the institution of slavery would later incite our only civil war and reach, more than two hundred years later, into our contemporary history only supports the importance of telling these "new" stories. Stress can be placed on the fact that all historical research is evolving and dynamic, subject to new research and scholarly debate. This ongoing process makes history interesting and engaging and keeps us returning to museums.

At a traditional plantation site, the white family made up a small percentage of those working and living there. It was not uncommon for a twelve-member family to have owned 120 slaves. Even at an urban site such as the Bellamy Mansion Museum, there were eleven family members and nine enslaved servants. To give the enslaved African Americans a brief interpretation and not include them in all areas of the house—in the family and formal as well as the work zones—is to turn a blind eye to who was doing maintenance and upkeep of the formal and family areas, making possible the traditional stories told in these rooms.

At one time, a common solution was to give parallel tours of the Euro-American and African American experiences. This addressed the concerns as to not cutting back on the established, traditional tour about the white family and kept the primary identity of the site as one of "Southern gentility." A separate African American tour meant that museums could check "inclusive tour experience" as part of their site description, yet still largely facilitate a tour of limited dimension. The daily, guided tour that most visitors took was changed only slightly, if at all, so that most people who came to the site heard little about the African American experience and its direct relationship to the prosperous family lifestyle depicted. Parallel tours make it too easy for visitors to sidestep contradictions or encounter any other story than the Euro-American one. Eichstedt and Small review this process and its limitations in *Representations of Slavery*.[13]

A holistic approach to interpreting the history of a site with inclusion of all who lived and worked there lends credence and authority to the interpretation. Providing additional side tours to focus more time on a theme referenced in a tour is also appropriate when a balanced main tour is achieved. For instance, at the Bellamy Mansion Museum, the regular daily tour, both guided and audio, describes the lives of the Bellamy family and the free and enslaved men, women, and children who lived and worked at the site. In addition, four times a year, the museum sets aside a Saturday to hold "African American History Day at the Bellamy Mansion," when African American history is the primary focus of the tour. Dovetailing with the site tours are demonstrations of and short lectures on African American history and folklife, as well as the lives and work of the free and enslaved artisan builders who constructed the buildings and on 1860s foodways, with a reenactment of the enslaved cook, Sarah. African American history is an important component in the regular daily tours, but highlighting this continuing work and alerting the public to the site's commitment to interpreting African American history are valid reasons for this special programming effort.

Revealing Hidden History

History that relates to difficult issues is often said to be "hidden." Not until 1995 did the National Park Service formally recognize, with signage at Fort Sumter, that slavery had contributed to the onset of the Civil War.[14] This federal institution, dedicated to education, had sidestepped the issue of slavery because it was such an emotional flashpoint.

Women's studies and women's issues encountered similar opposition and resistance in the 1960s and 1970s. Then, too, women's history was hidden and silent. Yet the roadblocks that appeared were not accepted as adequate deterrents. Research was done. Women studies departments were set up at colleges and universities. Historic sites presented women's history tours and programming. Now we see this as a normal part of telling history.

The truth is that a great deal of hidden history can be revealed. You can look into other sites doing similar work dealing with similar issues. As you explore a broader interpretation, look for what is unique about your site and what is similar to others to aid your research. Find what you can about other families in the area from the period, and work from there. Sites with African American programming listed online will reveal programming on broad topics that are not strictly specific to the site. Browsing sites on the Internet, I found lectures on what life was like for enslaved individuals in the Mid-Atlantic region during the late eighteenth century, building techniques and materials used by enslaved builders, and a local nineteenth-century African American whose primary achievements had taken place across the country from the site. These were all interesting programs but not narrowly specific to the sites. Be persistent, and be patient. Listen to your local educators, scholars, and librarians. Use online sources. Pick up the phone and call other sites. It is not that the information is easy to find and abundant but that there is enough information for you to work with in a responsible way with substantial results.

Developing the Interpretation

Bellamy Mansion Museum

Best practices can be achieved at a site even when the resources appear at first to be limited. Even the challenges of telling the difficult story can be used as a way to relay to the audience what the issues are, why they are important, and why they may be unfamiliar. The importance, as well as the difficulty, of including the Bellamy Mansion Museum's rare, intact urban slave quarters in the site's interpretation became apparent as the process began in early 2002. The building was not safe for inside tours and would have to be interpreted

Photo 2.2. The Bellamy Mansion Museum and Slave Quarters. (Courtesy of Madeline Flagler)

from the exterior. Some archaeological work had been done, but no final report had been prepared beyond a summary that was less than five pages. There was important research on the free, hired-out, and enslaved men who had labored on the construction of these buildings,[15] but not on the domestic slaves at the site. The most significant and usable information was from a four-year-old historic structure report.[16] This report was exhaustively but intriguingly detailed and became the single most important document in creating our interpretation of the lives of the enslaved servants. We also had two memoirs by Bellamy family members[17] who lived in the home before, during, and after the Civil War. These documents gave very little direct information. In the 1860 census, taken at the family home several blocks away six months before the family moved to its new home, we found the sex and age of the nine slaves (two adult men, three adult women, one teenage girl, and three young girls). By the next census, the Civil War had ended, and only three servants were listed at the home; of these, only one could be linked to the site during slavery. Church records showed nothing that we could relate to the Bellamys' enslaved servants. A will gave us the first names of a handful of slaves inherited by Dr. Bellamy. The unpublished memoir of a young architect who had worked on drawings of the house[18] rendered several sentences on a slave who worked on the construction of the house. The Bellamy family memoirs gave the names and sex of the slaves at the home and some ages. Two adult women and two men were listed with their jobs. There was no mention of the spousal or family relationships of the slaves on the site, except that one of the women was the mother of two of the three children. Some of the information between the census and the memoir did not readily match. Despite these challenges, we had more information than we initially thought: There were two family memoirs; the apprentice architect's memoirs; a handful of family letters; some photographs, deeds, and information in several secondary sources, including newspaper records; an extensive monograph on the family and house[19]; and a well-researched book published in 2004,[20] all concerning the Bellamy family and its history.

When we assembled all the direct information on the enslaved men, women, and children who had lived and worked at the site, we had three pages of typed notes. We had names, ages, and some occupations. We had no family or personal history and no physical descriptions. When I visited sites such as the Hermitage, which had actual slave lists and photographs of those who had been enslaved there, I was envious.

We did have the historic structure report and the intact quarters, so we could fully interpret the building and its construction. That story alone was fascinating, and it was a good beginning, but it did not achieve a fully dimensional picture of the lives of those who were housed there. Social history and building preservation are intertwined but remain two separate strands of information.

With the intent of having the restored building and the site interpretation work hand in glove, it is important to clarify the interpretive goals in reference to the restored building. A formal meeting on restoration goals for the Bellamy Mansion slave quarters established that restoration would strive to present the point of view of an enslaved person on that site in 1861. That restoration goal said a great deal about the institution's interpretative goals.

Site interpretation and restoration can aid or thwart one another. In the best of circumstances, they complement one another. From the historic structure report, we could discuss in the site interpretation what we could see directly from the structure and our knowledge of building techniques of the time, supplemented by the deed information and a fragment of one sentence in one memoir. The goal of relaying the point of view of those enslaved here was a helpful part of the framework as we put the interpretation in place.

We could also describe what we did not know and compare the building with others with parallel uses. We did not know how the rooms were furnished. We have no way of knowing whether the building had rustic furnishings or castoffs from the Bellamy family. We do not know what was on the floor or what was hanging at the windows. We could not say what the construction of the building indicated about the Bellamys' treatment of their slaves. We could compare and contrast the Bellamy quarters with those on other plantations and urban sites. We could note that while other quarters had bare, unfinished walls in spite of refined exteriors, our quarters had well-finished, plastered interior walls. We could note that of the sleeping spaces, all but one had a fireplace, and the one that did not was above the laundry and was likely warm all the time.

As we discussed the enslaved servants in the tour, here again, we could contrast what we did and did not know and why. We know some of their names from a memoir and can pair this information with the age and sex of some of them from the 1860 census. We have some occupations.

We could also describe why finding this information is not easy. Slaves were considered property. They were not listed in the census as full members of the household. No names were given, although they were for whites. They were listed by sex, age, and race. That is all. They did not legally own property, so they are not listed in deeds. They were not described in newspaper accounts or town records except by first name, if at all, and then in relation to criminal activity. We could describe the typical life of an enslaved servant in an urban setting in contrast with the life of an enslaved person who was a field hand. This segues into the diversity of slavery practice in an urban setting: those who were "hired out" worked away from the master's property; those who "lived as free" managed to live as free though no paperwork has been found concerning their freedom; "free blacks" had been born free or manumitted. In an antebellum city like Wilmington, each of these designations has an important story to tell. From research by Catherine Bishir, a noted architectural historian, and from the assistant architect's journal, we could identify from each of these designations men who had built the house and outbuildings. These men did not live in the quarters but were associated with the site. This information allowed us to describe in the tour an important facet of urban life in the South during this period.

With persistence and diligent research, we have produced a good, solid tour of the site that fully incorporates the experience of African Americans in Wilmington before 1865. It has been done without the ideal volume of documented information specific to the site but with a great deal of information on slavery in the cities and on plantations during the period of our site interpretation (1859–1865). This also leaves time and space to keep an appropriate interpretation of the Bellamy family history.

Mission Houses Museum

The museum was founded by the Hawaiian Mission Children's Society, a genealogical organization of descendants of Protestant missionaries, who arrived in the Sandwich Islands in 1820 to minister to the natives and convert them to Christianity. Interpretation that includes native Hawaiian perspectives has been well established at Mission Houses, but the issues of difficult history have not faded.

The museum's process of increased inclusion stemmed from a push to research more deeply the missionaries and the context of their lives in Hawaii. A watershed in reinterpretation occurred in the mid-1980s when the Mission Houses Education Department embarked on a process of research to put together more primary source materials on the Chamberlain family for a program at the site. As this project matured, information was assembled for use in schools. Local educators were then included in developing these materials, and their requests for fuller portrayals of the missionaries and life on the site led to inclusion of native Hawaiians and a wider cast of people in Honolulu.[21] The lives of native Hawaiians from royalty on down, as well as of the foreign merchants, sea captains, and other expatriates, were added to the interpretation along with the necessary historical and political contexts.[22]

Today, the three beautifully restored New England–style structures provide a pleasant visual respite in the middle of Honolulu. Situated in the historic Capitol District, they are only a block away from 'Iolani Palace and the Judiciary Building, where the Hawaiian government was overthrown by foreign businessmen, some of them the children of missionaries. All of these structures carry the mana and memories of significant religious, social, and political events that relate to the colonization of the independent Hawaiian kingdom. The discussion of Hawaiian sovereignty is activity debated today, much as it was during the time of the mission.

By the late 1990s, native Hawaiian scholars were included in discussions at Mission Houses concerning programming and interpretation. Sometimes this happened during more formal meetings at the museum; at other times, less formal discussions were held over a shared meal. There were meetings with leaders of Hawaiian *halau hula* (dance groups), taro-growing cooperatives, and Hawaiian language teachers, all groups who are deeply invested in promoting and preserving Hawaiian culture. Discussions resulted in programming, such as a Hawaiian-language festival and annual history days that included native Hawaiian components as important features, along with Civil War reenactors (Hawaiians served in the war) and quilt makers. In interpretation, there were changes to refurnishing and interpretation perspectives and a new historic structure report, all of which tapped heavily into primary resources. Vocabulary is carefully selected. Hawaiian words are used throughout the tours in their proper context. This is particularly effective when the English translation has a patronizing tone.

Mission Houses Museum is fortunate to have primary resource materials in its archives of missionary journals, account books, business correspondence, photographs, and paintings. For three decades, the education staff has presented a variety of living history programs, with reenactors portraying missionaries, native Hawaiians, Tahitians, African Americans, merchants, and seamen. Hawaiian and English are spoken in dialogue, and missionary women talk with members of tours about the oppressive heat, childbearing, and the dramas of communal living. Much of this programming comes directly from the volumes of mission journals. Native Hawaiians quickly became literate, publishing their own newspapers, editorial pamphlets, and broadsheets, providing documentation in their own hand. This contrasts sharply with the lack of first-person primary sources from the African Americans interpreted at the Bellamy Mansion.

Mission Houses traditionally had a candlelight tour at Christmas with reenactors in period clothing reading passages from the journals of the missionaries and their children. Some Native Hawaiian characters had been included in this program, but in 1999 we reexamined the candlelight tour to look at how to include more diversity. Not only were we able to able to give more dimension to some of the native Hawaiian portrayals, but we also included two African American historical figures who had been important in the early years of the mission: Anthony Allen and Betsey Stockton, both former slaves. Allen was a prosperous landowner and businessman who had greatly aided the mission in its first years. Stockton, a teacher, was a well-educated freed slave and the first single woman sent to this mission. Both Betsey Stockton and Anthony Allen had been featured as part of earlier African American History Month portrayals, but not as part of a more inclusive program.

Photo 2.3. Anthony Allen portrayal at Candlelight Christmas at Mission Houses Museum, 1999. (Courtesy of Michael Dunn)

Community Input

The importance of community input cannot be overstated. In Wilmington, we navigate the local history of the 1898 race riot and the 1971 Wilmington Ten. Both instances involved injury and death resulting from clashes over issues of political equality, economic dominance, and racial unrest. The horrors and trials of these incidents are not forgotten by the local community. The wounds have been addressed but have not healed. The Bellamy family's role in 1898 and the building's iconic Southern architecture looming over the main street, with its slave quarters in the backyard within view of the street, create a dual set of narratives and impressions within the local community that are invisible to outsiders. One impression is that of pride in the community's prosperous, antebellum heritage; the other is that of violent racial oppression. Mission Houses Museum, a mission site within two blocks of 'Iolani Palace, has similar emotional realities relating to local history. The missionaries were directly linked to the government of the Hawaiian Kingdom, and some of their descendants are linked to the uncompromising overthrow of the kingdom in 1893. Here, as well, local emotions continue to run deep.

To ignore or even sidestep these types of local issues is inauthentic and will undermine the interpretive goals you have set. These issues do not have to be central to your site interpretation but must be part of the docent training and provide an important context for local history. You also do not want your docents to be blindsided by difficult questions from visitors. With a little preparation, they can answer the concerns voiced and gently guide the tour forward. Community input can clarify how local history impacts the site and how you can address it to better serve the widest audience.

Once you have determined your statement of purpose and preliminary research, it is time to refine community input through an advisory board. As you look at addressing difficult issues of gender or race, your institution may wish to find board members from the communities in question. Mission Houses Museum and the Bellamy Mansion Museum actively recruited board members from the community as the first steps of this process were being taken. These board members can be the conduit for finding advisory board members who can help you develop an interpretation that addresses issues important to the community in a way that is sensitive to its concerns as they relate to the community's history and this site in particular. An advisory board comprising a broad spectrum of the community is imperative for success.

There is never one audience. There is never one female audience, one black audience, or one female black audience from one town. There are multiple audiences with multiple layers. Look to those who have a history of building bridges between these groups within your community. Look not only to educators but also to church, civic, and media leaders. At the Bellamy Mansion, as we began to address slave history with the still-polarizing backdrop of Wilmington's 1898 race riot, we looked to community leaders, public school educators, local pastors, and business people. If the strongest leaders were not available but interested in the project, we asked whom they would recommend. These important elders were then recontacted from time to time for their opinions as we looked for ways to address concerns. We found that some in the community, on both sides, did not want us to address the issues we felt were important. At times, it was hard to resist dismissing these naysayers out of hand, but the issues addressed in our interpretation concerned all segments of the community. When we addressed issues of slavery, we needed to understand that this history involved not just one constituency but several. Working with your board, staff, and community contacts using a team mentality and allowing leadership to develop and unfold at each step is important as you examine the questions asked.

Training Docents

The restructuring of interpretation through either tours or exhibits requires a staff, both paid and unpaid, that fully understands and supports the interpretation of not only the easy, traditional narratives but the more difficult issues as well. Docents and guides need to become not only familiar with new informa-

TEXTBOX 2.2

COMMUNITY CONTACTS

An example of the importance of community contacts occurred when we were planning an African American genealogy workshop. The Bellamy Mansion Museum had been doing African American programming for several years and getting some good coverage in the larger local newspaper. The black community was not attending in large numbers, but we felt this was a cultivation issue that would resolve itself. We knew there was great interest in African American genealogy, and 150 miles away lived the woman who a member of the local genealogy group described as the best in the state. I was told, "She is the one to get." I arranged for her to give a workshop at the local library. I sent out the press releases, made the usual contacts, and waited for the class to fill. A week before the class was to be held, I had five people signed up. I called an emergency meeting with my community contacts, and we considered our options. We were convinced that the date and time were good and that there was substantial interest in the subject. We did not want to bring Dr. White to Wilmington for an underattended workshop. In addition, we needed our fledgling program to be successful. What had gone wrong? As we talked, I learned that a small percentage of African American households subscribe to the local paper I had been contacting. I learned that most of the local African American community gets its information on local events through social organizations, e-mail lists, and churches. This was information I could never have discovered sitting at my desk. I took copious notes. We made detailed plans for rescheduling the event with contacts, time lines, and follow-up procedures. I listened, asked questions, listened some more, and took more notes. I rescheduled Dr. White with my deep apologies that, due to my inexperience, I had failed to make the contacts needed for proper publicity. Our group kept close contact through frequent phone calls, e-mails, and meetings and was able to execute the new plan for getting the word out. When Dr. White held her genealogy workshop three months later, we had sixty attendees with no paid advertising, just the right community contacts.

tion but engaged with a change they may not want. This frontline museum staff needs to be fully prepared not only to present the interpretation that has been developed but also to address the questions that will be asked as this complex, nuanced narrative is presented to the public. The time frame must be thought out to encompass the necessary changes fully.

An excellent framework for docent training for new tours that include slavery is described by Julia Rose in "Rethinking Representations of Slave

Life."[23] This PhD dissertation describes the transition as docents begin to move from a tour that has marginalized slave activity at Magnolia Mound Plantation to one that gives the slaves at the site a multidimensional portrayal that allows them to be fully seen as individuals. Rose lays out a series of education and discussion sessions that aid in restructuring the docents' perceptions of the site and its inhabitants.

In dealing with difficult issues, vocabulary must be examined and words carefully chosen. Listen to your community leaders and watch their use and choice of words to describe your goals and intents. As you develop your training, alert your docents to word choices when they are giving tours and speaking with the visitors. At the Bellamy Mansion Museum, we were careful to use the term "sleeping room" or "sleeping space," not "bedroom," in the slave quarters because the word "bedroom" has a different connotation for today's visitors. It implies a place of comfort, privacy, and leisure, all of which have no application to the concept of slavery.

The reinterpretation at the Bellamy Mansion Museum began with a series of lectures and walkabouts with our docents. They were given copies of research notes and asked for feedback and questions. It was important for them to feel that we were building this interpretation together. They needed to feel vested in the process and to ingest the information gradually. The lectures were not required, but attendance was high, and several came to all the lectures, even when some were repeated. We brought in local scholars to address questions and expand on information in the training materials. This gradual process spanned three years and is ongoing. A key ingredient was the stories of the individuals who lived and worked in these spaces. Their stories would catch the interest not only of the docents but also of visitors.

The story of Sarah, the enslaved cook, intrigued us from the beginning. We had her name and occupation from a memoir.[24] We determined her age from a census record that included only her gender, age, and race. The memoir stated that she remained at the mansion to look after it when the Bellamys left town during the Civil War, and she served at the site when it was used as a Union headquarters after the city fell. That was all we had. But we could describe the life of an enslaved cook: her workday, responsibilities, hierarchical relationship to other slaves on the site, and work relationship with the family. We could use information on foodways of the period and describe how they changed during the Civil War in relationship to the blockade of the city by Union ships. We could use what we knew about the life of an urban slave in a wealthy household on the eve of the Civil War.[25] We could describe the exodus of skilled free slaves to the North in search of a better life. We could describe the life of those who stayed. We were able to fill out her life enough to give her a persona of depth.

We had no personality or physical description, but we had enough to impart a sense of who she was.

Living history has its own set of obstacles in interpreting difficult issues. Asking someone to portray frequently caricatured historical figures, such as enslaved people, can be uncomfortable for program directors, and the portrayal itself may be a difficult challenge for some to accept. The week that I started at a site as education director, there was a reenactment that included the representation of a slave. I had not been in on the planning process and did not know the actors. One actor, dressed in period clothing, was bantering behind the scenes before the event began. I realized I had not discussed the goals of the program with him, and his level of discomfort and ambivalence were already interfering with what we wanted to achieve. We spoke and were able to express our views of what was about to happen at this site in this portrayal. We found common ground in the perspective of this as an opportunity for him, as the actor, and I, as the director, to give dignity and humanity to a role often portrayed, at best, one-dimensionally and, at worst, through simple caricature. His discomfort gave way to confidence as his sense of how the role could be best interpreted was verbalized. He and I worked together over the years, creating fine performances we were both proud of. I learned the lesson of valuing the actor's perspective and being clear about the end goal of a thoughtful, respectful interpretation.

Historic site interpretation of tough issues is not edutainment; it is programming dealing with a subject that has been poorly handled in the past and remains very emotional. It must be approached with thoughtfulness and respect by every participant. Overseeing programs and listening to all the participants for clarity requires dedication. The children who are acting parts need to be just as informed as the adults as to what they are doing and why. Sites need persistence in continuing work with each program, patience as comfort levels are worked toward, and listening to hear concerns and confusion.

As you look for actors or reenactors, realize that each role requires sensitivity and a comfort level. Local acting groups are natural places to look for your actors. Our community has a couple of African American acting groups that have been a great resource. Local storytellers and musicians have contributed richly to interpretation. But some of the best actors come from unexpected corners. Some skill and an emotional understanding of the subject matter go a long way here. There was an art teacher who brought student groups four times a year from a small town fifty miles away for a field trip to the Bellamy Mansion Museum. In the spring rains and the winter ice, she brought one of her four classes each quarter. After working with her during these field trips for three years, I asked her if she would be interested in coming to the site and portraying Sarah, the enslaved cook. She was hesitant because of her lack of acting experience, but

Photo 2.4. Sulnora Spencer as Sarah at Bellamy Mansion Museum, 2008. (Courtesy of Ann Hertzler)

we both believed that her interest in the subject and her skill as a teacher would make up for her lack of formal acting skills. We put together a costume, and I gave her notes and background reading. We had some good conversations and put the program together. I brought in fresh foods that were appropriate for the period and season, and the site had its first African American History Day. Raised in Chicago, but teaching art in rural North Carolina, this very special woman, Sulnora Spencer, became the heart of the program. She spoke for us on camera for the media and posed for TV and newspaper cameras; when we were asked by the state history museum in the state capital to do an African American cooking segment for a family day, which neither of us had done before, we worked together to create another successful program.

Dynamic Settings

In 1991, in New York City, the unexpected discovery of a few bones in the middle of the city spurred research that resulted in an exhibit, book, and national dialogue about the presence of slavery in parts of the United States not traditionally recognized for deep involvement in both owning and trafficking in human beings. History, by its very nature, is dynamic. It is a social science. It is social because it is about people. It is a science because, as we dislodge old concepts and disprove traditional theories, we make progress. Reexamining interpretations and making changes to tours that have become integral to a site's identity is a time-consuming process full of all types of roadblocks. Yet professional interpretive standards require that the process be ongoing. New viewpoints, new research, and new dialogues keep museums energized and vital. Women's history; African American, Native American, and native Hawaiian history; working-class contributions and struggles and their importance to who we are as Americans—all are threads that were long considered minor and insignificant to the American fabric. They are now seen as important and necessary, even vital, to authentic, accurate, and professional interpretation in history institutions.

Recently, our local public radio station used the phrase "We are not a museum" to promote its institution as one of energy and new ideas. The station was emphasizing that it is not dusty and stuffy. I was unsettled. Museums *are* spaces of energy and new ideas. They are spaces where uncomfortable dialogues can be addressed and meaningful exchanges of ideas and information are regularly part of the experience. It requires persistence, patience, and listening but interpreting tough issues is rewarding. It can broaden your audience, deepen your community involvement, and ultimately contribute to sustainability. We *are* a museum, and we *are* vibrant contributors to the fabric of our community.

Acknowledgments

I wish to acknowledge Deborah F. Dunn, who shepherded me through my first experiences with interpreting difficult issues and has been helpful and supportive in her suggestions concerning this chapter.

Notes

1. Barbara Tuchman, *Guns of August* (New York: Ballantine Books, 1994), 463.
2. Deborah Dunn, telephone conversation with author, March 2, 2010. Dunn has been executive director at Mission Houses Museum and 'Iolani Palace in Honolulu, Hawaii.
3. Susan P. Schreiber, "Interpreting Slavery at National Trust Sites: A Case Study in Addressing Difficult Topics," *Cultural Resources Management* 23, no. 5 (2000): 49–50.
4. Donna Ann Harris, *New Solutions for House Museums: Ensuring the Long-Term Preservation of America's Historic Houses* (Plymouth, UK: AltaMira Press, 2007).
5. Jennifer Eichstedt and Stephen Small, *Representations of Slavery: Race and Ideology in Southern Plantation Museums* (Washington, DC: Smithsonian Institution Press, 2002).
6. Julia Anne Rose, "Rethinking Representations of Slave Life at Historical Plantation Museums: Towards a Commemorative Museum Pedagogy" (PhD diss., Louisiana State University and Agricultural and Mechanical College, 2006). Dr. Rose is currently director of West Baton Rouge Museum, Port Allen, Louisiana.

7. Rose, "Rethinking Representations of Slave Life."

8. Dwight T. Pitcaithley, "Public Education and the National Park Service: Interpreting the Civil War," *Perspectives* (November 2007), www.historians.org/perspectives/issues/2007/0711/0711pro2.cfm.

9. Robert S. Starobin, *Industrial Slavery in the Old South* (New York: Oxford University Press, 1907), 10.

10. Interpretation Standard 2, *StEPs Workbook* (Nashville, TN: AASLH, 2009), 110.

11. Dunn, telephone conversation with author, March 2, 2010.

12. Schreiber, "Interpreting Slavery at National Trust Sites."

13. Eichstedt and Small, *Representations of Slavery.*

14. Pitcaithley, "Public Education and the National Park Service."

15. Catherine W. Bishir, Charlotte V. Brown, Carl R. Lounsbury, and Ernest H. Wood III, *Architects and Builders in North Carolina: A History of the Practice of Building* (Chapel Hill: University of North Carolina Press, 1990).

16. Peter Sandbeck, *Bellamy Mansion Slave Quarters: Historic Structure Report*, Vol. 2: *History, Documentation and Paint Analysis* (Wilmington, NC: The Museum, 1998).

17. Ellen Douglas Bellamy, *Back with the Tide* (Wilmington, NC: Bellamy Mansion Museum, 2002), and John D. Bellamy, *Memoirs of an Octogenarian* (Charlotte, NC: Observer Printing House, 1942).

18. Rufus W. Bunnell, "The Life of Rufus William Bunnell," Bunnell Family Papers, Sterling Library, Yale University.

19. Diane Cashman, "History of the Bellamy Mansion" (research report presented to the Bellamy Mansion, Inc., 1990).

20. Catherine W. Bishir, *The Bellamy Mansion—Wilmington, North Carolina: An Antebellum Architectural Treasure and Its People* (Raleigh: Historic Preservation Foundation of North Carolina, 2004).

21. Conversation with Deborah Pope, executive director of Shangri La, Honolulu, Hawaii, on March 3, 2011. Pope was at Mission Houses Museum from 1978 to 1994, serving in the education department and then as executive director.

22. John A. Herbst, "Historic Houses," in *History Museums in the United States: A Critical Assessment*, ed. Warren Leon and Roy Rosenzweig (Champaign: University of Illinois Press, 1989), 106–9.

23. Rose, "Rethinking Representations of Slave Life."

24. Bellamy, *Back with the Tide.*

25. Richard C. Wade, *Slavery in the Cities: The South, 1820–1860* (New York: Oxford University Press, 1977).

THE TRUTH, THE WHOLE TRUTH, AND NOTHING BUT THE TRUTH: RESEARCHING HISTORICAL EXHIBITS

Teresa Goforth

Museum exhibits tell stories in the most compelling and fascinating way. They pull people to them through sights and sounds and the promise of "the real thing." They provide visual context to a multitude of rich stories that, without the work of small museums all over the country, might not otherwise be told. An exhibit may be beautiful and exciting, but without solid, diligent historical research as its foundation, it jeopardizes the trusted status of the museum within the community. Museums have a responsibility and an obligation to present only the most accurate and current information to their audiences. Visitors trust museums to provide them with "the truth," insofar as that is possible, and all museums must honor that responsibility. To do so requires a passion to dig for clues and piece together the facts that make up the stories that combine to create the fabric of our communities. Museum exhibit research is a great adventure.

This chapter provides you with stepping-stones for successful exhibit research. You will learn some basic definitions of types of research sources and, through a series of textboxes interspersed throughout the chapter, follow the research development of a small museum exhibit as it might happen in real life. It is important to note that, as with most other aspects of museum work, there is no single right way to accomplish the end goal of a well-researched, truthful exhibit.

Where to Begin?

The adventure begins with an idea, which can be inspired by many sources. Sometimes, as the director or board member of a small historical museum, you spend time wandering through the collections storage areas surveying the beauty and intrigue of it all. Perhaps you have an interesting group of objects that can tell the story of an important person in the community, or perhaps some curious items, such as interesting agricultural or household articles, can illuminate activities of times past. Those objects might be the starting point of your research adventure. For example, a small museum in rural Michigan has a large collection of objects that either are elephants or contain images of elephants. There is an entire dinner service, figurines, costume jewelry, and much, much more. These objects belonged to the first Michigan woman to run for the U.S. Senate, Elly Peterson. A prominent member of the Republican Party, she received many of these items as gifts from friends and supporters. The staff knew these objects would be of great interest to the museum's core visitors and so, from the inspiration of this one group of artifacts, developed an exhibition exploring the political history of the county, including, but not limited to, this single person.

Inspiration might also come from the community. All of our communities have people who are passionate about their own history, and that passion often manifests itself in the collecting of objects and the pursuit of research about specific topics. Perhaps there is a commemorative event for the community, a bicentennial or celebration or memorial of an event. These are great opportunities for museums to reflect their communities, to take part in the activities that bring community members together, and even to grow their collections. That same small museum mentioned above had the opportunity to celebrate an event that embodied community spirit. The town commemorated its centennial in 1963 with a giant celebration for which much of the town dressed in faux nineteenth-century attire; commemorative wooden nickels, a full-color book, and other accoutrements were produced. Roughly thirty-five years after this event, the museum chose to do a temporary exhibition about the centennial celebration during its more modern annual festival. It was able to show objects only exhibited on rare occasions and to make a call for other objects still in private hands in the community. Many of these objects were donated to the museum once the exhibition ended, and, perhaps most exciting, a film of the original event that most members of the community had never seen came to light.

Finally, exhibit topics may be inspired by information gathered by the person in the museum who acts as curator, the content expert. This person ideally brings together collection and community to determine exhibit topics. He or she has a solid understanding of the needs and interests of the museum's visitors and develops topics that both meet those needs and support the museum's mission.

Regardless of the source of inspiration, the exhibit cannot become a reality without diligent research and development. This chapter outlines the steps and resources needed to accomplish this fundamental task.

Sources: What's What?

Before moving on to talk about how to do historical research for the purpose of museum exhibition, it is critical to spend a little time providing some basic

BY THE STEPS 1: CHOOSING A TOPIC

Museum XYZ, a small museum in a rural county, has a paid staff of one, numerous committed volunteers, and a board of directors. It develops and presents a new exhibition to its visitors every year. The museum's director is a part of the local Rotary Club and participates in activities with the chamber of commerce, the women's club, the local library, and other community organizations. In her time in the community, she has learned of a long history of interesting women, and she knows the museum has the collections to support an exhibition about women in the community. The board of directors and volunteers include a significant number of women, all of whom are excited about the topic and agree that it would find great support in the community. It is formally proposed to the exhibitions committee and scheduled for the changing exhibit space the following year.

definitions of resource materials. It really takes all the types of sources to create an accurate, comprehensive story for your exhibition.

Primary Sources

Primary sources are materials written or produced during the period under study and often provide us with the most valuable information related to a subject. A primary source has not been analyzed or interpreted by a third party; rather, it is a direct reflection of the person or period being researched. Examples of primary sources include diaries and journals, newspapers, letters, business ledgers, and census documents. Starting with primary sources gives the researcher the opportunity to take a step back in time and view events from the perspectives of contemporary players. They can often be inspirational in the development of themes or a story line for an exhibition.

For the same reason that they are useful, they must be read and utilized with care. We have a great advantage as historians: We often have fifty, seventy-five, or even hundreds of years of perspective, new research, and learning to inform our knowledge of historical events and periods. This allows us to view them with a greater objectivity than if we were living at the time. The same holds true for the present. Historians eighty years from now will have a much better perspective for understanding the events of our lives than we do. That said, primary sources are invaluable tools for understanding history when used in conjunction with modern information and scholarship.

Secondary Sources

Secondary sources are those materials written about history, using primary sources as a foundation or evidence for the research. Modern authors, not those contemporary to the period or event, generally write them, and they can be great resources for locating primary sources for a topic, as well as other secondary sources. Examples of secondary sources are textbooks, monographs, and journal or magazine articles. As with primary resources, it is very important to read them critically and to ask questions. Do not always accept an author's word at face value. Ask yourself if his or her argument has been supported with primary documentation in a way that makes sense. Historical research is about critical thinking.

Unearthing Context

Once the inspiration is clear, the exhibit has been approved by the proper channels, and you are ready to move ahead, it is time to clarify the story, to understand the overarching themes and ideas and determine the context into which the local story will be placed. Even when you are telling a local story, be it of a community, county, or state, it is important to understand what is going on around the subject to give the story context. The first step in researching the exhibit, once you have a topic, is to take a little time to read up on the period at hand. College history textbooks are an excellent resource for understanding the broad themes of various historical periods. (Many college professors post their class syllabi online, listing the textbooks they use in their classes. A quick Internet search for "Intro to U.S. History syllabus" will provide you with numerous options. Inexpensive used editions of the books can generally be found at booksellers' websites, such as Amazon.com or Bookfinder.com.) Once you have a text, read the chapters relevant to the period you are researching and then ask at least the following questions:

- How did the larger events of this time in history affect the people of the period presented in the exhibition?
- Are there events or topics that we, the exhibit team, did not think of in relation to the exhibition content?
- Is there new material in the textbooks? Or does the secondary literature contain topics that might form useful sections in the exhibition?

Once you have spent some time learning about the historical context and answered these questions, it is time to move on to the second layer of secondary literature research. A monograph, as defined by Merriam-Webster, is "a written account of a single thing."[1] It is a nonfiction book about a single subject. For example, Deborah Gray White's *Aren't I a Woman? Female Slaves in the Planta-*

tion South is a monograph. A textbook covers many topics, generally over a significant amount of time, whereas a monograph focuses on a very specific topic. The next step in your research process is to seek out useful secondary literature in monograph form, if available, so that you can delve more deeply into your subject matter. Finding monographs on a particular topic is just like searching for any other kind of material, but you might have trouble getting them at a local bookstore. You will have the most success using the online library catalogs of major universities. In most cases, anyone can access those catalogs, and you can then request the title using interlibrary loan at your local library.

TEXTBOX 3.2

BY THE STEPS 2: UNDERSTANDING THE CONTEXT

In thinking about their exhibit about women in the community, the members of the exhibit team determine that its topic should be a little more focused, and they decide to look at the daily lives and accomplishments of women in the community between 1840, the period of settlement, and 1920. This is the period best supported by the collection, and it will frame an exhibit small enough to not overwhelm the visitors and large enough to allow the team to provide more stories and detail. So, the research must begin, and the team takes the following steps:

- The director pulls a handful of U.S. and women's history textbooks from her shelf and shares them with members of the exhibit team.
- Team members are encouraged to read the chapters for the period from 1840 to 1920 and to make notes of important events as well as information directly related to the history of women.
- When the team reconvenes, members have noted that important themes for the period include agriculture, the Great Awakening or religious revival, ideas of social reform (e.g., schools and prisons), the growth of the antislavery movement, progressivism, and the suffrage movement.
- Choosing those themes most relevant to the subject at hand, the group seeks out a few monographs to give them more detail (e.g., *All-American Girl: The Ideal of Real Womanhood in Mid-Nineteenth-Century America, Women in the Civil War*). The titles depend on the priorities set by the exhibit team.

Perhaps one of the most useful aspects of the monograph is the opportunity to use its bibliography. In adventurous terms, it is like a treasure hunt. While the modern analysis of the subject is enlightening, the list of other resources in the bibliography of the monograph, both primary and secondary, leads you on the chase to the "truth" of your topic. Monographs provide you with more puzzle pieces to assemble to tell your story.

Organizing Ideas: Multicolored Index Cards Are Awesome!

Now you have a mound of contextual material that you must somehow turn into a coherent museum exhibit, accessible to a diverse audience. In order to make that happen, and before you move on to collecting local historical resources, it is an excellent idea to organize your thoughts into the main ideas of an exhibit, if you have not already done so. Ideally, you have determined along the way what the main message of your exhibit will be. The initial research process should have given you some ideas about what the various sections of the exhibit will look like. They might simply be chronological, but they also might be thematic, covering the major events and issues you have determined relevant through your initial research.

Without getting too far into logistical details, a great way to brainstorm and physically organize your thoughts and ideas is to devote some wall space to the project if you can find it. Using multicolored index cards, assign a different color to each potential section. Put the exhibit section headings on the wall. On each subsequent index card, write a piece of information discovered during your research that supports that particular topic. Eventually, as you move through the local research to refine the topic into a local history exhibit, you will add thoughts from that research, object ideas, photos, activities, and so forth. This creates a wonderful physical manifestation of the research you do, which can be both refreshing and practical, as the research can sometimes feel intangible and overwhelming.

Technology: The World at Your Fingertips

The technology of today has changed the face of all historical research, but particularly local research. Whether you live in a large city or a small, rural community, you can now access books, documents, and other resources from your living room couch or your local coffee shop by using the Internet. While it is still necessary and, yes, fun to sit in reading rooms in the basements of libraries and historical societies searching for nuggets of useful and exciting information to assemble your puzzle, much of the legwork can be done from almost any-

TEXTBOX 3.3

BY THE STEPS 3: GREEN IS FOR AGRICULTURE

The team now knows its exhibit on women in XYZ county from 1840 to 1920 will be organized thematically. Through contextual research and conversation, it has decided to include the following themes as sections of the exhibit:

- Women on the farm
- Women and the church
- Women and reform
- Women and leisure

Now that these themes are in place, the director assigns each a color: green for the farm, yellow for the church, orange for reform, and pink for leisure. Team members put a sticky note or card as a heading on the large wall cleared for the purpose, leaving a great deal of room between the columns for other sticky notes or cards. Now the team takes all the contextual pieces of information it has, writes each idea on a card of the appropriate color, and places it on the wall under the corresponding heading. This process continues as the team gathers more detailed exhibit information and includes cards that indicate a photograph or an object for the exhibit.

where. Archives, libraries, genealogical societies, and museums have digitized their catalogs, so not only can you look to see who has what, but in some cases you can actually see the what, without ever leaving your computer, expediting the research process. This also means that you can very quickly get a more comprehensive understanding of what exists in the country to assist your research efforts. Prior to the advent of this technology, traveling to each physical location was a necessity to find what you were looking for. This was expensive both in terms of time and money.

If you are not comfortable with technology, find that volunteer in your community who lives to seek out obscure things online. Those individuals are out there, I promise. And they can help you find the many indexes for online resources now available on the Internet. Exploring these Web resources will help you narrow down your research directions and limit the number of physical visits you will make, opening up doors to resources you may not have known existed.

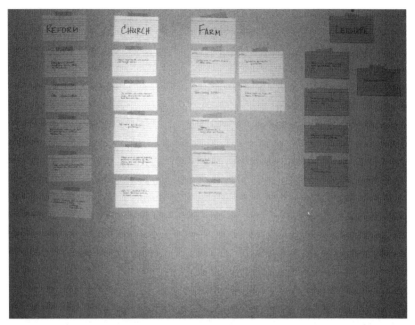

Photo 3.1. Example of an arrangement of colorful index cards used to organize thoughts and ideas that will become exhibit content. (Courtesy of Teresa Goforth)

TEXTBOX 3.4

BY THE STEPS 4: TECHNOLOGY OPENS THE DOOR

The exhibit team is in the midst of researching women's history and decides to tap technology to see what returns. This is only one example of many. Over about a two-minute period, an exhibit team member types "women's history local index" into a Google search box and returns a plethora of Internet links. The first link clicked takes the team member to the National Women's History Project. An obvious link on the home page reads, "Links." This yields a very refined list that relates specifically to women's history and research. Among the categories that come up is "Resources by State." This is a great start. While looking for the links area, the team member sees that the site also has mini-biographies and summaries of the lives of women in various historical periods and as they relate to specific events. All this happens in two minutes. Imagine the resources an hour could provide!

Making It Local: What Are the Resources?

By completing the contextual research, an exhibit team has the framework within which to place its local story. The team can now ask the following questions:

- How do the historical stories of the people in our community fit into the context?
- How do their stories reflect this larger context?
- How are their stories different?
- Do these local stories provide a different perspective on the events and issues of the broader context?

These questions can help guide the quest to research and document these local stories. Sometimes, the local story is more difficult to research than the national context because so little has been written at the local level, and what was written forty or a hundred years ago is often based as much on hearsay and folklore as on the historical record. I talk about these sources later because, despite their shortfalls, they can still hold great value as clues to the past for the researcher.

No one knows better than the museum's staff and volunteers the research resources available in the museum or its archives or at the local library or genealogical society. The first step in making those resources speak to the content of the exhibition is to gather a comprehensive list. The resources might take many forms: photographs, letters, journals, diaries, county histories, plat maps, and publications developed and created during the time in question. It is good to know where each is housed (e.g., at the museum, the library, the genealogical society). This list might include the state archives or state museum as well. Most state archives have at least some component of their collections available on their websites. Some may only have the catalog digitized, but for many, at least some of the collection is actually viewable online. For example, the state of Michigan has its Civil War materials, including photographs, letters, and diaries, scanned and available on its website. This includes transcriptions of the letters and diaries. The Mississippi State Archives has a number of its photograph and government document collections available to online researchers as well. State archives also often maintain microfilm of local newspapers. It is important to remember that some local resources are no longer housed within the physical boundaries of the community.

Diaries and Letters

The greatest treasures of research for nearly any historian are letters and diaries. They are the expressions of the players themselves, their personal thoughts and ideas as they react to the world around them and interact with their communities. In some cases they are writing for others' eyes, but, as with a diary or journal, most are writing for themselves only; thus, they provide an insight for the historian that might not be found in a public correspondence. Letters and journals can provide content support for the exhibit as well as the content itself. Quotations within the texts of these documents might suffice as large graphics for the exhibit or simply form important parts of the exhibit label, allowing visitors to see or hear the local characters speak for themselves. This is very powerful when we talk about one of the museum's most important qualities: authenticity.

When using letters and diaries as historical resources, you must ask a few important questions:

- For whom is the author of the letter or diary writing? It is important to know this and to know something about that person to make sure you have the opportunity to think about motives and ways in which a relationship between the two individuals might inform what is being written in the letter. For example, if you are working on an exhibit about the Underground Railroad in a particular area, and you are reading a letter known to be written by a landowner whose property served as a stop on the railroad, knowing to whom he is writing is critical. If he is writing to someone in the community not sympathetic to the work of the Underground Railroad, the content of that letter may not reflect completely accurate feelings or information.

- If the source is a diary, do you have any sense of whether the writer intended for the words to be read by someone else, or was the diary intended to be a private affair? As with letters, if diarists know that someone will read the writing later—for instance, elected officials or famous individuals might assume that their papers will be of interest in the future—they may censor themselves for the potential audience. If written privately, a diarist's words are apt to be much more candid.

- Are there potential pitfalls in using certain private correspondence? This question must be answered on a local basis. Are descendents of the writer still alive in the community? Will release of certain pieces of information ruffle feathers among the public that the museum serves? An answer of yes does not necessarily mean that the museum should not use that resource. Rather, it means the museum should proceed carefully and be as accurate as possible.

Photographs

Photographs are another invaluable research and exhibit tool for historians and museums. While they can be used for illustrative purposes as objects in an exhibit, they can also provide excellent information about a person, an environment, and a context. For example, a nineteenth-century photograph of someone sitting in her parlor gives great insight into the way interior spaces were furnished and decorated at that time. It helps to understand the objects important in a person's life and the value placed upon them. Photographs of a downtown building might help identify past businesses or perhaps even objects housed in the museum's collection, like a light fixture or a sign.

As with letters and diaries, it is always important to consider context and think critically about subject matter when using a photograph for an exhibit or for research. You must ask the following questions:

- Who took the photograph?
- Where was it taken?
- Is it a candid photograph, or was it staged? In other words, were the subjects unaware that they were being photographed, or was the scene set up and organized by a photographer to enhance composition or the drama of the shot? The practice of doctoring photographs to change the content or context is not new. It has been happening since the early days of photography.[2]
- What can I see in the photograph that is not the focal point? What is in the background? Can the photograph provide additional information that I did not expect to find?

County Histories

A preponderance of county histories was published in the United States in the latter half of the nineteenth century, perhaps as a response to the nation's centennial but more than likely as part of an effort to document the settlement and survival stories of the county's early residents as they began to pass on. These histories have titles such as *The Past and Present of Eaton County: Historically Together with Biographical Sketches of Many of Its Leading and Prominent Citizens and Illustrious Dead* and *History of Hampshire County, West Virginia, from Its Earliest Settlement to the Present.* These tomes can be found in nearly every U.S. state, if not all of them, and can provide valuable basic information to assist in exhibit research.

As with all sources, some caution must be exercised with these works. Their celebratory nature sometimes means that the history they provide is somewhat superficial. They were intended to celebrate the great citizens of their respective counties, not necessarily to look critically at the history of the area. Therefore, some of the more difficult or controversial issues are absent. This is often particularly noticeable in the accounts of settlers' interactions with the American Indians present in the area when Europeans arrived. This is not to say that these histories are not useful. On the contrary, they generally provide useful biographical information and a general overview of the founding of an area and its communities. But they should be used in conjunction with other sources.

More modern histories are written as well, often by museum volunteers and longtime community residents. Again, as with any source, think critically when using these for research purposes, and ask the following questions of the author's work:

- Did the author document the primary resources on which the book is based? If so, take a little time to spot-check some of those sources; see if you would have the same interpretation. If the author did not document primary sources, then you must use the work carefully as a basis for your research because you cannot independently verify the authenticity of the information presented. This is not to say these sources are not valuable, just that we have to look at them, like all sources, with an analytical eye.
- Was the book created for a specific purpose (i.e., was it written for the chamber of commerce or other marketing organization as a souvenir or as a piece to be used to encourage people to visit the community)? Like the nineteenth-century county histories discussed earlier, these can be more celebratory and not necessarily a comprehensive history of the community.

Public Documents

Public documents should not be ignored as important sources of information. Sometimes they are mined only for more empirical data or statistics, but they also can lead you to other useful stories. Public documents include census records, deeds, wills, court records, and other legal documents. These are usually located in county government offices, but occasionally, if the documents have been microfilmed or digitized, the original documents may be located in the state or county archives or in a local museum.

It is important, if possible, to look at the original documents. County court documents in the nineteenth century were roughly legal-sized documents that were then folded in thirds, with the pertinent information written on the outside of the document. In some cases, when looking at the original, you will find interesting bits of information written on the outside of the document, offering insight into the more personal aspects of the data contained within. For example, while doing research for an exhibit, I ran across some documents that were letters of indenture from the court for children from the county superintendant of the poor to local farmers for service on the farm. In return, farmers were to provide clothing, shelter, and education to the children. On the outside of one of the indenture letters was a note that the child's mother had attempted to retrieve her child from one of these farms. That small note lends great insight into the emotional and human aspects of this kind of government transaction that will not come through the standardized legal documentation contained within.

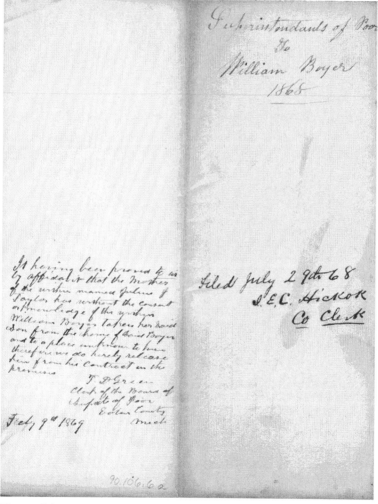

Photos 3.2. Legal document from the superintendent of the poor in a mid-Michigan county. Writing on the outside tells the story of a mother taking back her indentured son. (Courtesy of Julie Kimmer, Courthouse Square, Charlotte, Michigan)

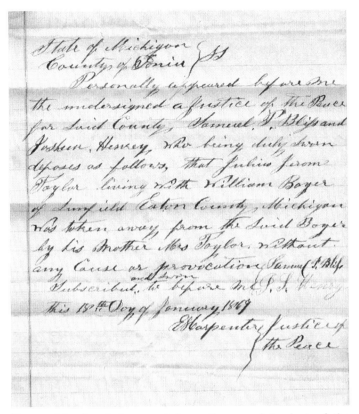

Photos 3.3. Legal document from the superintendent of the poor in a mid-Michigan county. Part of the story is told outside the formal portion of the document. (Courtesy of Julie Kimmer, Courthouse Square, Charlotte, Michigan)

Oral Histories

If presenting an exhibit for which the players in the historical story are still alive, you can create a new historical source by conducting oral histories with those subjects. Oral history is not an endeavor to take lightly. In and of itself, it requires research, but it also requires a great deal of thought and preparation, recording equipment, time, and planning. There are many resources to help you work through an oral history project, one of the most informative being the Oral History Association (www.oralhistory.org), but often state libraries, archives, and genealogical societies can help as well.

Undertaking an oral history project has an immediate research benefit and a long-term one as well. It provides firsthand accounts of the subject at hand, but it is also a tool for gathering information that, if done well, will leave a rich historical legacy for the museum. The following are basic components of a successful oral history project:

- Have a plan that includes a finite research topic. Oral history is not successful if you go in without a focus for your research. If you intend simply to ask your subjects to tell you about life in your county in the 1930s, you will get hours of tape with a lot of information but little substance or focus. If, however, your plan is to gather information about attending a one-room schoolhouse in the 1920s or being a soldier in France during World War II or participating in civil rights demonstrations in the 1960s, you will mine much more substantive information for the future.

- Once you have a clear topic on which to work, develop specific questions about that topic to ask those you are going to interview. The questions should be consistent from interview to interview, but this does not preclude you from asking follow-up questions to clarify answers.

- It is extremely important that you make sure to have a consent form prepared and to train all volunteers to have the interviewee sign it. This is a critical step in the interview process. Without the consent form, you may not be able to use or reproduce the interview in the future! A sample consent form is available at the following address: www.oregon.gov/OPRD/HCD/.../Oral_History_Interview_Consent_Form.rtf.

- Make sure you provide training for all staff and volunteers who will be conducting interviews. While some elements of interviewing are straightforward—ask a question, get an answer—others are not. Interviewers may need to be reminded that in some cases the information they are asking these individuals for is personal and can be emotional or sensitive. In addition, the questions may indirectly ask interviewees to reflect on someone close to them, a friend or a family member, which they may not want to do. Train interviewers to not press their subjects too hard; it will often cause them to stop talking. Respect their privacy and emotions, and be sensitive. You may have the opportunity to go back to those questions and get answers—or you may not.

- Doing oral histories requires some form of recording equipment. When choosing that equipment, you need to think about standardization and longevity. The oral history association can help you choose audio and video equipment. It has a page on its website devoted to the different types of technology and their advantages. It is imperative to make sure staff and volunteers are trained to use the equipment and that it is checked to be in working order before each and every interview. There is nothing worse than sitting down for an interview and finding out your battery is dead or that you do not have the correct cable.

- Once the interviews are complete, it is important to have a plan in place to transcribe and index them to make them even more effective as research tools.

The Nebraska State Historical Society created an excellent online oral history primer (www.nebraskahistory.org/lib-arch/research/audiovis/oral_history) to guide those undertaking such a project through the process, the logistics, and the pitfalls.

While all these resources come in very different forms, they can each provide pieces of the puzzle you are trying to put together as the foundation of a museum exhibit. Probably most important when looking at any of these sources is to examine them with a critical mind. Do not take any source at its face value. In order for the source to really speak to the researcher, the researcher must ask difficult questions about the source. It is that questioning that truly enlightens the subject.

What Is the Object?

"Objects embody unique information about the nature of man: the elucidation of approaches through which this can be unlocked is our task, the unique contribution which museum collections can make to our understanding of ourselves."[3]

At the core of what history museums do, be they large or small, is the collection of objects. Our missions all involve preserving the collection and interpreting it for our visitors or using it for educational purposes. So far, we have looked at the plethora of sources available for contextual research for an exhibit. Now, we must look at the object and how to utilize it as its own historical source. It is hard to believe how many stories a single object can tell.

Interpreting Objects

When you choose objects for your exhibit, you have a general idea of the part of your story they will tell, but now it is time to delve a little deeper. Look at each object, and just as you did with the documentary sources, ask and answer these questions about it:

- When was it made?
- How was it made?
- Who made it?
- Why was it made?
- How was it used?
- Who used it?
- What can we tell about the time during which it was created?
- Would it be created today?
- How would it be used in a story?
- What stories can the object tell?
- How could a person today use this object?

Answering these few questions gives us opportunities to use a single object in many different ways. As we take stock of our stories and our objects, because we have thought about them critically, it is possible to think about them in different contexts and move them around in an exhibit to where they are best able to help tell the story.

Researching Objects

Just as we research context, we must also sometimes research objects to interpret them to their full potential. This research as a bit different from the contextual research outlined earlier. Some sources are very particular to object research. Some of the greatest resources for identifying common historical objects are historic catalogs, such as those for Sears, Roebuck & Co. and Montgomery Ward. Reprints of various editions, mostly from the late nineteenth and early twentieth centuries, are available for between $10 and $15, so they are very accessible even to the smallest museum. They are particularly useful because of the breadth of objects they cover. For example, when cataloguing the textile collection in a very small museum, we were having trouble accurately identifying various women's undergarments. One look through the Sears catalog from 1895 gave us accurate terminology. From the same catalog, we were able to identify historic kitchen tools and agricultural implements. These resources should be on every small historical museum's bookshelf. Many other resource books are helpful for identification as well, some of which are listed in the resource list at the end of this chapter. There are also specific handbooks on the market for identifying American Indian artifacts, as well as collector's manuals used by antique dealers.

Sometimes you make object identifications by happenstance, just by keeping your eyes and ears open as you read state history magazines, peruse newsletters

BY THE STEPS 5: ANALYZING AN OBJECT

One of the objects the exhibit team chooses for its exhibit on women in the community is a quilt that has been in the collection for many years. At face value, the team knows the quilt can help illustrate the work of women and craftsmanship, but it can tell so much more. Here are the questions the team asks and the answers:

- When was it made? It was made in the 1880s.
- How was it made? It was made by hand. Pieces of fabric were sewn together in a pattern, layered with cotton batting and muslin backing, and quilted together. It is a sampler quilt; each square is different, and a different name is embroidered on each square.
- Who made it? By the names on the squares and a patch on the back, we know the quilt was made by a women's group in the community of which we have excellent records.
- Why was it made? A little research through the museum archives turns up minutes from this women's organization. The quilt was created for auction to provide support for a local charity for the poor.
- How was it used? We know from the donor that it has remained in the family that won the nineteenth-century auction; it was used on beds and eventually displayed in the home.
- Who used it? The winner of the auction was a member of the woman's organization and the wife of a prominent businessman in the community.
- What can we tell about the time during which it was created? From our research, we know that women's organizations around the country were taking notice of various reform needs in society, particularly with regard to women and children in poverty. This local group reflects that national trend.
- Would it be created today? Yes, absolutely. The museum has an associated group that makes and raffles a quilt annually to support the museum and other charitable causes.
- How could it be used in a story? It could be used to talk about quilting as a necessity and a pastime, about women's organizations and their role(s) in the community, and about the many ways women participated in progressive reform movements in the late nineteenth century.
- How could a person today use this object? It could be used for display or functionally.

Now that team members have thought about these questions, they can reevaluate where in the exhibit the quilt will work best. It could be used in the "Women on the Farm" section to talk about the ways women spent their time for work and for pleasure, or perhaps it might tell a more interesting story in the "Women and Reform" section.

from other historical organizations, and interact with members of the community. For example, when relocating a large cast iron stove in our small museum, we opened the oven to discover a number of objects stored inside, including an oddly shaped device. It had two long, narrow wood pieces, hinged at one end with a brad of sorts, which had a bent wire piece on each of the other two ends. The name of a local hardware store in the community, long closed, was imprinted on one of the narrow wood pieces. We really had no idea what this object could be, despite looking through catalogs, antique identification books, and so forth. One day, the state history magazine came in the mail, and on the front cover were photographs of a number of odd objects, including this strange object found in the stove. The magazine identified this strange little object as a "pie puller." Women used them in their kitchens to pull pies from the oven so they did not burn their arms reaching in with potholders. The fact that the local hardware store name was printed on top suggests that this object was more than likely a premium given away with a purchase. This kind of information can come from conversations with visitors and through publications and really just requires an attentiveness to unexpected but useful information.

Regardless of how you identify objects, taking the time to get as much information as possible can only enhance the story you tell in your exhibit. Knowing what the object does, who made it, and who owned and used it leads to a more complete, better-illustrated story in your exhibit.

The Legacy of Your Research

The hard work expended to research an exhibit is not wasted energy. It is important to organize and file the research notes and even a bibliography for the future. The museum is bound to do an exhibit in coming years with parallel stories to tell, and if you have maintained your files well, some of that hard work may already be done for the next exhibit.

TEXTBOX 3.6

BY THE STEPS 6: IT ALL COMES TOGETHER

The exhibit team's hard work culminates in the resources necessary to take "Foundations: The Women of XYZ County, 1840–1920" from the page to the walls and three-dimensional spaces where it will invite visitors to explore, experience, and learn. Each diligently researched section has been designed to bring out the themes, ideas, and facts that have been uncovered. The community is invited to share in the adventure by attending a grand opening, including a presentation by a woman who has made significant contributions to the community and beyond its borders. The exhibit team members, board of directors, and members of the community get to celebrate the exhibit together. In addition to viewing the exhibition, visitors have the opportunity to scan a list of the oral histories and artifacts newly acquired by the museum to find their own connections to the subject, beyond the exhibit.

In the end, the exhibit brings new visitors to the museum, is utilized by the local school district in its social studies curriculum, and inspires other members of the organization to start thinking about future exhibition ideas. All of the research materials from the exhibition are filed and made available for future research and exhibitions. The city council acknowledges the museum for its important contribution to the culture and legacy of the community.

Conclusion

Researching exhibits is a great adventure, but it also involves a tremendous amount of work. It requires diligence, critical thinking, creativity, and excellent organizational skills, and, perhaps most importantly, it is imperative to the overall success of any exhibit. Our great responsibility to our visitors to maintain authenticity and objectivity mandates that we be diligent in researching our exhibits. Technology and access to information have leveled the playing field between large and small history museums in their ability to be comprehensive in their research, limiting the need to travel and allowing researchers to be more creative in the search for sources. The rewards of this work are great, and the trust it develops between the museum and its visitors is a significant part of the muscum's making itself an integral part of its community.

Resources

U.S. History Textbooks

These textbooks with varying perspectives are often used in general U.S. history courses. Hundreds more are available.

Jones, Jacqueline, Peter H. Wood, Thomas Borstelmann, and Elaine Tyler May. *Created Equal: A History of the United States.* 3rd ed. New York: Longman, 2008.

Norton, Mary Beth, David M. Katzman, David W. Blight, Howard Chudacoff, and Fredrik Logevall. *A People and a Nation: A History of the United States.* 7th ed. Florence, KY: Wadsworth Publishing, 2004.

Roark, James L., Michael P. Johnson, Patricia Cline Cohen, Sarah Stage, and Susan M. Hartmann. *American Promise: A History of the United States.* 4th ed. New York: Bedford/St. Martin's, 2008.

References for Object Identification

Bragonier, Reginald, and David Fisher. *What's What: A Visual Glossary of the Physical World.* Maplewood, NJ: Hammond, 1990.

Corbeil, Jean-Claude, and Ariane Archambault. *Macmillan Visual Dictionary.* New York: Macmillan, 1997.

Sears, Roebuck & Co. and Montgomery Ward catalogs, with editions from many different years, are available from many online booksellers, such as Amazon.com.

Organizations

American Association for State and Local History (www.aaslh.org)
Oral History Association (www.oralhistory.org)

Statewide Museum Associations and Field Services Offices

Most states have a museum association that offers programs and resources to help small museums. To locate a field services office in your state, visit www.aaslh.org/FSA/FSA .html. These organizations can usually facilitate the answering of questions by putting you in contact with other museum professionals who are generally very happy to help.

Libraries

Local libraries are amazing facilities—conduits to the rest of the world. As they are sometimes located in rural communities, the number of titles related to the work of museums and historical research is often limited. However, because so many libraries now participate in lending networks and can use interlibrary loan services, patrons in all parts of the country have access to just about any title they desire. Nearly all university libraries have online catalogs where you can browse titles. Request those titles from your local library's interlibrary loan program, if possible.

Websites

Online County Histories, Biographies, & Indexes—USA (www.genealogybranches
.com/countyhistories.html): This website is a comprehensive genealogy listing, providing many resources by state. It includes historic county histories and biographies,
among other resources.

History Matters: The U.S. Survey Course on the Web (www.historymatters.gmu
.edu): History Matters, while created for students and college history teachers, makes
available a great number of primary documents and resource materials that could be
adapted for use in exhibit research and even in exhibit-related educational programs.

Notes

1. Merriam Webster online entry for "monograph" at www.merriam-webster.com/
dictionary/monograph.

2. See "Phototampering throughout History," Dartmouth professor of computer science Hany Farid, www.cs.dartmouth.edu/farid/research/digitaltampering (accessed May
3, 2011).

3. Susan Pearce, ed., *Interpreting Objects and Collections* (London: Routledge Press,
1994), 125.

CREATING EXHIBITS: FROM PLANNING TO BUILDING

Eugene Dillenburg and Janice Klein

What Is an Exhibit?

A museum exhibit[1] is, at its most basic, a medium for communicating information, and like all forms of communication, it has its own defining characteristics. Understanding the features that make exhibits different from other forms of communication makes it possible to take full advantage of the unique opportunities a museum provides for presenting information.

Table 4.1. Unique Characteristics of Museums

Museums Are . . .	Good Exhibits Are . . .
Free-choice experiences—visitors decide which exhibits or sections of exhibits they will see	Built for success—make the trip worthwhile by creating situations where the visitor is likely to see the point or complete the task
Physical spaces—visitors walk through and are surrounded by the exhibit	Strongly dimensional—they have objects, props, and other three-dimensional components, and also make use of the total environment, including the visitor path
Open to a broad audience—visitors bring a wide variety of abilities, knowledge and learning styles	Relevant and accessible to the general visitor and support diverse interests and learning styles
Multimodal—exhibits engage different senses (sight, sound, touch) and have different types of expression	Engaged with multiple modalities and take full advantage of the different senses employed during a visit
Nonlinear—visitors do not take a predetermined route, but choose their own path	Clearly organized—the structure of the information is transparent, easy to follow, and can be understood in any order
	Strongly focused—present and reinforce a single clear message
Temporal experiences—the visitor sees different parts of the museum or exhibit over time; however, most visitors have an informal "time budget" and generally spend twelve to twenty minutes in a gallery	Designed so individual components can stand alone, and don't require the visitor to have seen something else first; however, together they create a cumulative effect
Social experiences—visitors often come with family and friends	Designed to accommodate more than one user, designed to encourage conversation and/or group activity

Exhibits serve multiple purposes for museums. They are, first and foremost, a vehicle for informal public education using the objects collected and preserved by the museum, props, interactive devices, and other three-dimensional pieces. However, exhibits also provide an appropriate atmosphere for programming, increase museum attendance and revenues, raise the institution's prestige, and provide a place for social interaction.

In general, a well-structured exhibit is clear, always focusing on a single message. It is organized in a way that makes sense to visitors and helps them understand the content. And finally, the exhibit conveys information not through words on a wall but through objects and experiences in a space.

The process of creating exhibits is often divided into three or more phases, including content development, design, and installation. In larger institutions, these are usually carried out in an overlapping sequence by different members of staff. In smaller museums, however, a single staff member often creates an exhibit from beginning to end. Additionally, smaller exhibits may be developed in a nonlinear form, with modifications made in content or design as the exhibit is installed. For these reasons, this chapter focuses on the activities required to create an exhibit without necessarily placing them in a strict sequence.

Topic

The exhibit process begins with the identification of its topic or focus. There is a wide range of exhibit topics; inspiration may come from the collection itself, upcoming special occasions in the community, or the opportunity to collaborate with another institution. New acquisitions can be used to provide a new or expanded context for older parts of the collection. For example, the Mitchell Museum of the American Indian used the donation of a substantial collection of Northeastern U.S. Indian beadwork as an opportunity to create "Peoples of the Great Lakes," an exhibit that included the museum's extensive basketry collection as well. Similarly, the hundredth anniversary of the birth of the museum's founder allowed it to bring all the objects in the founding collection together from their different locations throughout the galleries.

Since exhibit ideas can come from a variety of sources both inside and outside the museum, one way to ensure the broadest possible input is to create a mechanism for the ongoing or periodic compiling of exhibit ideas. This can range from an exhibit suggestion box to regular community meetings. It is also important to have a formal review system in place to make sure the appropriate criteria are met and to provide a way of saying no. Formal approval of exhibit topics by the director or a board committee is one way to ensure this.

Finally, the exhibit topic should also be in keeping with the museum's mission and fit its interpretive goals for exhibits (see Standards and Excellence Program for History Organizations [StEPs] Interpretation Standard 2 and chapter 1 in this book). In forming these goals, the museum should make sure to include

- a purpose—that is, a broad statement of what the overall exhibits program will achieve;
- a general area of subject-matter focus;
- a general description of the audience the museum wishes to serve;
- a description of what is exhibited (e.g., the museum's own collections or material borrowed from other institutions or from local collectors);
- an enumeration of how many permanent installations there are in the museum and how many are temporary, as well as how often the temporary exhibits change;
- a process—that is, a description of how exhibits are developed, who is involved, and how responsibilities are assigned.

Audience

After settling on a topic, the next step in the exhibit process is defining the audience. No exhibit will appeal to everyone. "Everyone" is not interested in every topic. "Everyone" does not have the same knowledge, skills, and learning styles. The more clearly the audience can be defined, and the more tailored the exhibit is to that audience, the more satisfying the visitor experience will be.

Audiences can be defined in three ways. First, there are demographic factors, like age, sex, ethnic background, income, household size, and education level. Certain topics may be more relevant to specific groups, and certain approaches may be more appropriate for particular audiences. Next, geographic factors revolve around where the audience lives. While small museums predominantly serve their local communities, there may be times when an exhibit is designed to focus on a particular area within that region or, alternatively, to attract seasonal tourists or those visiting from out of town. For example, the Mesa Historical Society developed an exhibit on the Arizona Cactus League for visitors who came during baseball spring training. Finally, psychographic factors include visitors' interests and motivations for attending. Will they be experts or novices on the exhibit topic? Is the exhibit intended for school groups on field trips or families wanting to do something together? Does the exhibit have a strong emotional appeal, perhaps commemorating an event in the town's history, or does it have more interest on an intellectual level?

While not all museums undertake formal visitor surveys, most do know who their regular visitors are. Exhibits can be designed to strengthen the museum's connection to core visitors or to attract new audiences. Being aware of potential audiences can also provide additional directions for exhibit content or programming. While the Mitchell Museum of the American Indian's exhibit "Winged Messengers: Bird Imagery in Native American Art" focused on objects from a variety of Indian cultures, it also included information for the local bird-watching community and a raptor demonstration.

Visitor studies can help focus the message, content, and design of the exhibit. Research need not be complicated to be helpful. At the Arizona Science Center, a single staff member asking visitors questions over just one weekend found that much of the center's audience for an exhibit on the history of the Phoenix area was relatively new to the region and primarily wanted to know why people would settle in such a hot and dry climate.

Visitor studies can provide an outside perspective to answer questions the exhibit team might have. When planning an exhibit on Pacific coral reefs, some staff at Chicago's Shedd Aquarium wanted to focus on sharks, arguing that this would be of greatest interest to the visitors. Others felt that coral was the center of the ecological story and that sharks were a tangent and should be treated as such. A survey found that visitors had high levels of interest in both sharks and coral (as well as whales and tropical fish). The team realized it did not face an either-or proposition: There was enough visitor interest to keep the exhibit centered on coral and also to justify the inclusion of a significant shark story.

Visitor studies can also affect design. Staff working on an evolution exhibit at the Field Museum worried that visitors would skip past the early sections, which contained the fossils that seemed small and undistinguished to the non-specialist, and head right for the big, flashy dinosaurs. On paper, the designer first planned a winding exhibit path, forcing visitors to slow down in those areas and potentially frustrating them. However, surveys revealed that most visitors expressed interest in those early sections. The designer drew a new floor plan: a straight hall with a series of rooms off it. He felt comfortable providing a clear path to the dinosaurs once he felt assured most visitors would indeed take the time to explore all the rooms.

Observations once the exhibit is in place may also guide your design. A beadwork exhibit at the Mitchell Museum of the American Indian included information responding to two common questions: Where did native people get glass beads, and what did they use before they had them? It soon became clear that the exhibit case containing the information about these topics was in the wrong place, since visitors were often heard voicing those very questions well before they came to the answers. A quick reorganization of exhibit materials solved the problem.

While some of these examples come from larger museums, the same lesson about the value of visitor studies applies to smaller institutions. The best way to discover your visitors' interests is to listen to them. The exhibit can then be developed to include responses to questions you know visitors already have.

Main Message

The next step is to identify the main message or, as Beverly Serrell describes it in her book *Exhibit Labels: An Interpretive Approach*, the "big idea." This is usually a single sentence that summarizes the exhibit content. It is the visitor's take-home message, and every component of the exhibit should reinforce this point in some way. Even though visitors may only view some components or see them out of sequence, they will be exposed to the main message several times within the exhibit and, through this repetition, may absorb its point. The main message, as written, may never appear in the exhibit, but it should influence every object choice, every label's text, and every design decision.

Serrell recommends that a main message contain a subject, an active verb, and a consequence—for example, "Rocks and minerals reveal clues to our planet's history," where "rocks and minerals" are the subject, what they do is "reveal," and the consequence of that revelation is understanding "our planet's history."

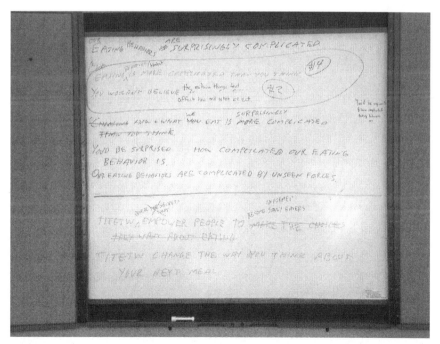

Photo 4.1. A main message brainstorming session, with several versions and a record of the editing and wordsmithing that went on. (Courtesy of Eugene Dillenburg)

The main message concept is important for two reasons. First, it identifies what to say, where to start, what to emphasize, and where to elaborate. Second, and more importantly, it also identifies what not to say. Any given topic could fill an entire book—in most cases, multiple books. But an exhibit has limited space, limited objects and text panels, and limited visitor time and attention. Focusing on the main message provides a tool to cut away the extraneous material and make the tough in-or-out decisions.

The medium of the exhibit, with its self-directed audience and nonlinear pathways, presents great challenges to clear communication, especially of complex subjects. Unless the exhibit has a good main message, clearly expressed and supported throughout, visitors will be unlikely to understand the point. Instead, they will probably view the exhibit as a room full of random objects rather than as pieces of a coherent story adding up to a single take-home message.

An exhibit without a clear main message is either stuffed to the gills with objects and information, because there was no mechanism for saying no, or a random hodgepodge of miscellaneous items, because there was no theme to tie them together. Either way, it will not communicate clearly, and visitors will get little out of it.

TEXTBOX 4.1

EXAMPLES OF A MAIN MESSAGE

"Sharks are not what you think." (Monterrey Bay Aquarium)
"What is it about dogs that makes us love them so?" (Los Angeles County Museum of Natural History)
"Everything changes, all the time, at speeds too fast or too slow for us to perceive." (Science Museum of Minnesota)
"During the Industrial Revolution, Americans harnessed natural forces and simple machines to build canal systems for transporting goods and materials cheaply." (National Canal Museum)

In each case, these simple statements give a clear indication of what the exhibit will say, how it will say it, what sorts of objects and experiences the visitor can expect, and even the "attitude" the interpretation will take. Each has its own emphasis: The shark exhibit will challenge misconceptions; the dog exhibit will strive to make an emotional connection with the audience; the time exhibit will surprise us; and the canal exhibit will focus on forces and machines as opposed to the many other things it could discuss.

Developing Content

Developing exhibit content includes both intellectual and physical aspects: the story line and the supporting objects, photographs, maps, and materials.

One area that poses difficulties for smaller museums is determining who will be involved in deciding exhibit content. Many books on exhibit development advise consultation with staff, volunteers, community members, and special advisory groups, as well as brainstorming sessions and audience surveys. For a small museum with limited resources, these activities can take more time and manpower than the museum can afford. (Textbox 4.2 describes how to conduct a brainstorming session that includes several people in developing exhibit content.)

It is important, however, to make sure the process is as inclusive as possible (see StEPs Interpretation Standard 3). If the exhibit focuses on a particular part of the community, the perspectives and beliefs of that group should be considered. Accuracy and authenticity are both important (see StEPs Interpretation Standard 4). However, sometimes including more voices in the process increases the likelihood of conflicting views and interpretations. Out of respect for both the participants in the planning process and the audience, it should be clear from the onset who will be making the final decisions (e.g., museum curator, director, project leader). Sometimes strongly held cultural beliefs and oral tradition must be carefully balanced with Western scientific or academic research. For example, in an exhibit on Navajo weaving, the Navajo belief that this group has always lived in the Southwest conflicted with historians' analysis that the Navajo migrated from further north and arrived in the Southwest in the fifteenth century. In cases like this, it is best to identify the source of the information (e.g., "Navajo oral history teaches . . .").

Once a sufficient number of ideas about content has been gathered, whether through formal consultation or informal discussion, a smaller group or single individual can begin to organize them, identifying what materials and ideas seem to go together, what groupings emerge, and what does not seem to fit. This process generally involves a fair amount of negotiating, striking a balance between objects, two-dimensional materials, and interactive components. There will be compelling reasons to include each type of content. However, it is important to remember that no exhibit can include all the information on a topic. The ultimate goal is to provide visitors with a coherent selection of relevant information rather than a dissertation or "book on the wall." Additional materials, including where the visitor can learn more, can be provided through handouts or on the museum's website.

Objects

Objects, of course, are the primary medium through which most museum exhibits communicate. They can be used to tell any number of stories, depending

TIPS FOR DEVELOPING CONTENT

Keep the group small. Having more than four to six people makes it hard to give everyone a chance to be heard, especially if some are reluctant to speak in groups.

Remember that everyone is equal. It can be intimidating to voice ideas in front of everyone, particularly for volunteers or community members. Make sure that everyone understands the rules. Sometimes it helps to have someone other than museum staff run the meeting.

Put the topic and main message up on the wall as a point of reference, but do not limit discussion in any way. Some people may come up with very specific ideas for an object or a point of information they think should be in the exhibit. Others may come up with grand, overarching themes and unifying threads. Both are important and welcome.

Write everything down, no matter how seemingly crazy. Do not worry about relevance, practicality, or even affordability at first. An idea that may initially seem off the wall may, after some discussion, start to make sense. Or it may inspire another, more achievable idea. Most importantly, do not criticize. Criticism kills creativity and erases equality. At this early point, quantity of ideas is more important than quality.

Have a time limit: Forty-five minutes to an hour is about all most people can manage. Do not worry if the perfect idea does not arise. You may want to hold another session or just review all the ideas with a smaller group.

Most important of all, have fun. If you do not enjoy yourself while making the exhibit, how can you expect your visitors to enjoy themselves while viewing it?

on whether the focus is on objects' physical attributes (aesthetic), their context (totemic), or a combination of the two (didactic).

Viewing an object aesthetically focuses on its formal attributes; there is no reference to context or broader meaning. Typically, such discussion emphasizes the appearance, age, or shape of the object. Some art exhibits, like those on classical sculpture or Chinese porcelains, choose to focus on the objects' aesthetic meaning. The exhibit aims to generate an understanding or appreciation of the objects themselves, divorced from any cultural or historical context.

The totemic approach is just the opposite: It is all about context. Within the story line of the exhibit, the object has no particular value in and of itself;

Photo 4.2. Results of a content brainstorming session, with ideas scribbled down onto pieces of paper and tacked up on the wall. Colors coded for different types of experiences: objects, interactives, media, and so forth. (Courtesy of Eugene Dillenburg)

rather, it represents some bigger idea. The classic example is Abraham Lincoln's hat. The hat was mass-produced, a common item for its time. It tells us nothing about the man, other than possibly his hat size. But Abraham Lincoln wore this hat! As a direct, physical link between the visitors and one of the most important figures in American history, it can be used as the starting point for many other Lincoln stories.

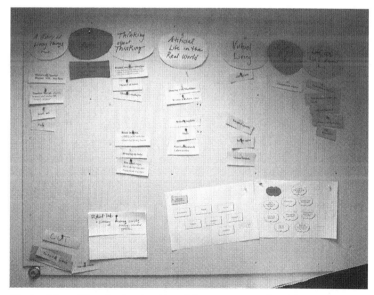

Photo 4.3. After brainstorming, ideas are organized into groups to create a storyline. Notice the "CUT" pile in the lower left corner—very important. (Courtesy of Eugene Dillenburg)

The didactic approach combines these two. Specific physical properties of the object are used as a springboard to discuss more abstract contextual ideas. A dinosaur bone has formal aesthetic properties of shape, size, and contour. These show where the muscles were attached, how big they were, and how the animal moved; thus, they describe the animal's role in the context of its ecosystem.

Of course, a single object may carry more than one of these meanings in an exhibit. For example, many natural history museums display large collections of mounted butterflies, arranged by size or color. This illustrates both the butterflies' visual features (an aesthetic point) and their biological diversity (a didactic point).

Similarly, the same object, in different displays, can mean different things. A stuffed beaver alone in a case is a display about the beaver. Add a woodchuck, and now the beaver is part of a "Rodents of the United States" exhibit. Take out the woodchuck and put in an aardvark, and the message becomes "mammals of the world." That same beaver in a case with a heron becomes "Michigan wildlife."

Two-Dimensional Materials

In addition to their role as objects with distinct individual meanings, two-dimensional materials, such as maps, photos, archival documents, drawings, charts, and diagrams, can provide important supplemental information. Maps are clearly important for exhibits that rely on geographic references, while a good diagram can take the place of paragraphs of explanatory label text.

Photographs can show objects or activities that are too large to fit in a case or even the museum, such as an image of a Hopi woman replastering her adobe home or a Civil War cannon. Photographs can also take the place of objects that may be unavailable or beyond the museum's resources to display properly but that are key to the story line, like an image of a woman in full Victorian dress. Especially effective is the juxtaposition of an object with an image of it in use—for example, a nineteenth-century Winnebago beaded hair wrap next to a photograph of a contemporary powwow dancer wearing a similar piece.

Hands-On, Audiovisual, and Interactive Devices

More and more museums are using hands-on, audiovisual, and interactive devices to engage visitors and support multiple learning styles. Museum objects, for all their glory, can generally only be viewed, not touched or moved. Touchable components engage more of visitors' senses and thus more of their brains.

Nonaccessioned objects or modern-day replicas placed on "touching tables" are the most common and simplest type of hands-on materials. Raw materials, like porcupine quills, buffalo or deer skins, and birch bark, provide excellent hands-on supplements to exhibits on Native American culture. Samples of local rocks and common fossils do the same for a geology exhibit. Clearly identifying these as noncollection items helps visitors understand that the museum maintains appropriate standards for the care of its collection and does not allow accessioned objects to be handled.

The addition of sound, whether as background music or specially recorded spoken text, is most easily done using a CD player. Short videos can be shown on a repeating loop or restarted by a staff member when appropriate. It is generally necessary to cover the control area of the CD or video player so that visitors are not tempted to change the settings themselves.

Interactive components, which have the visitor do something, like press a button or lift a flap, work best when the activity itself reinforces the message. For example, putting flappers over a picture of the local environment and posing the question "Where do hummingbirds live?" makes lifting the flappers an act of searching, which is exactly what a naturalist trying to answer that question would do. The activity becomes part of the answer.

There is no hard-and-fast formula for when to use an interactive as opposed to some other exhibit device. Two good questions to ask are as follows:

- Is the content important? Of course, everything in the exhibit should be pertinent and relevant. But some things are more central to the story than others. Interactives take time to plan, money to build, and staff to maintain. It is best to focus those resources on the most important points.
- Is this a good way to present this content? Some information is best illustrated through an object, a photograph, or a text panel. It may not be a good fit for an activity, and trying to make it active just for activity's sake will confuse and obscure the point. On the other hand, some ideas are difficult to communicate through static means, especially those that are physically big, conceptually abstract, or dynamic in nature. These are often better suited for an interactive approach.

Interactives do not have to be expensive. Some simple examples include

- graphics mounted on boards that slide past one another;
- overlays printed on acrylic;
- oversize maps laid out on the floor;
- models to put together;
- drawers that open to reveal additional objects;
- mounted magnifying glasses showing detail of small objects.

The Phoenix Museum of History used a miniature wooden wagon and appropriately sized beds, clothes trunks, tools, sacks of flour, and other necessities that would have been taken on the journey West to give visitors the opportunity to decide which of the many objects they would choose to put in the allotted space in the wagon. On a somewhat larger scale, the Tempe History Museum provides bins of plastic vegetables, small wheelbarrows, and wooden crates that allow visitors to "pick" and "pack" typical crops and load them into the back of a 1940s pickup truck. Each of these activities gives the visitor the opportunity to compare, measure, and get perspectives not provided by objects in cases. More ideas and step-by-step instructions for many interactives can be found in the Cheapbook series published by the Association of Science-Technology Centers.

More complex interactives, like touch-screen computers, are generally beyond the skills of small museum in-house staff or volunteers and may require the assistance of outside vendors. Two sources for these vendors may be found at the Museums USA (www.museumsusa.org/vendors) and AAM Marketplace (www.museummarketplace.com) websites.

Whenever possible, an interactive should be tested with visitors before the exhibit opens to see if they understand how to use it and what it means. A cheap model can be made out of cardboard and tape, and the interactive can be easily changed if it does not work.

Research

Exhibit research not only ensures the accuracy of what is said (StEPs Interpretation Standard 4) but can also suggest new ideas and approaches to improve the exhibit. Research on a model of the Roosevelt Dam for an exhibit at the Arizona Science Center uncovered that it was created by a well-known sculptor; use of that fact encouraged visitors to see the model not only as a technical representation but also an art object.

Research on a specific object's provenance will ensure that it comes from the right location, culture, or period. Research may also show that a selected object is not appropriate for the exhibit or that some other item illustrates a content point better. Such changes are common in the exhibit design process and generally result in a richer, more tightly focused story. Depending on the topic and institutional resources, information can come from in-house expertise, external advisors, or reputable published sources. (See chapter 3 in this book for more information on exhibit research.)

Exhibit Organization

The information in an exhibit needs to be organized. Visitors will be unable to make sense out of an exhibit if ideas and objects are presented in a random fashion.

In general, the individual components of an exhibit can be organized by time, by category or theme, or by location. Less commonly, content can also be effectively organized hierarchically (e.g., biggest to smallest) or even alphabetically. An exhibit should be organized by one of these schemes, and one of the most important steps in exhibit development is carefully selecting the scheme that best conveys the exhibit message.

Most history exhibits are organized by linear time, telling the story of a town, county, or other region from its founding up to the present day. Other exhibits present time as cyclical, describing the hours of a day, the seasons of a year, or the steps in a process. For example, "Amazon Rising" at the Shedd Aquarium in Chicago takes visitors from the annual dry season to the rainy season and back again.

However, arranging an exhibit chronologically presents several challenges. First, the exhibit's "present day" soon becomes the past. It is necessary to continually update the exhibit with more recent materials so that it does not become outdated.

Next, while most people easily understand the concepts of before and after, they may not be able to follow a long or complicated story laid out as an exhibit. Many people have trouble keeping time straight on scales longer than a human lifetime. They may understand the distance between "my childhood" and "Dad's childhood" and even "Grandpa's childhood." But the distance between Grandpa and Abe Lincoln or between Lincoln and Shakespeare is harder to gauge. A simple time line can help visitors comprehend exhibits organized this way.

Finally, the purely chronological approach can pose problems when presenting multiple perspectives in the same exhibit. The Bob Bullock Texas State History Museum is organized chronologically but also aims to tell the story of all Texans, including African Americans, Indians, Hispanics, and women. Every period room contains some panel or display about each of these groups. This means that a visitor who is interested in, say, black history in Texas has to go through the entire museum, room by room, looking for the one panel in each that talks about the subject. The content is not all gathered together in one place.

One way to deal with some of the problems of the chronological approach is to organize the exhibit by category or theme. The Minnesota History Center is able to include multiple perspectives in its exhibits by organizing them around themes like work, transportation, music, and weather and comparing the past with the present in each.

The notion of the category, however, has its own challenges. Experts think about their subjects in terms of categories: They divide broad topics into specialties. Museums also generally organize collections by category, often to aid experts in their study. However, the categories used by experts to understand the world are often very different from those used by the general public. The zoologist sees the mackerel as a fish, the dolphin as a mammal, and the crab as a crustacean. The nonzoologist may simply group all these together under the heading "sea life." It is important that the categories used to organize an exhibit match the visitors' categories, or can at least be easily explained to them. Visitor research or discussion among staff and volunteers can provide insight into generally understandable terminology.

An example in which familiar categories are not used is the American Museum of Natural History's dinosaur halls. One is dedicated to the order Saurischia, the other to the order Ornithischia. While this is a clear paleontological distinction, it is not terribly helpful to the parent whose ten-year-old child wants to see the tyrannosaurus and the triceratops, now in separate rooms. And while most visitors probably understand the difference between birds and mammals, or between warm-blooded and cold-blooded animals, the distinction between artiodactyls and perissodactyls (even- and odd-toed, hoofed mammals, respectively) is not likely to be particularly meaningful to anyone not already a zoologist.

Since an exhibit is a physical space, location can be a particularly powerful method of exhibit organization. Objects and other exhibit components are arranged and arrayed spatially in the gallery. If the story line is also organized spatially, with different information tied to specific real-world locations, then the organization of the display itself carries meaning.

As with time, there are many ways for location to be used in exhibit design. A planetarium or astronomy museum may organize itself as a trip through the universe, the galaxy, or the solar system. Many collections can be organized by world geography, by continents or countries. Regions, states, or neighborhoods in a town can also be used if these are the stories the exhibit aims to present or contrast.

Location can also work well on a smaller, more human scale. Many museums re-create street scenes and organize displays within different types of buildings or businesses. A historic house is naturally divided into rooms. You can get smaller still, "shrinking" your visitor down to explore the human body or the parts of a computer.

Labels

Content

Museums most commonly communicate their messages and interpret their objects through the written word—that is, labels. These are often broken down into four levels:

Table 4.2. Types of Labels

Exhibit or Gallery Label	• Explains the main message
	• Draws the visitor into the exhibit
Section Label	• Used when there is more than one case or component about a specific part of the story
	• Provides an overview of that section of the exhibit
Case or Component Label	• Summarizes the content in an individual case or component
	• Connects to and elaborates on the main message
	• Explains why these objects are grouped together
Object Label	• At its most basic, identifies the individual object with title or name, but can include more detailed information (e.g., date, provenance, and museum catalog number)
	• Provides detailed information or background on a specific object
	• Gives instructions for an interactive device

Headlines—that is, full sentences or phrases with a noun and verb—are commonly used in label writing both to summarize panel content and to encourage the visitor to read the whole text. Since studies have shown that most museum visitors

---

TEXTBOX 4.3

SAMPLE CASE LABEL

Dolls, miniatures, and other toys allowed Native American children to learn adult skills as they had fun.

Children's first toys were usually given to them, but once they could carve, sew, and bead, they were expected to make their own playthings. Accuracy was important even in making toys. As children grew older, their craft skills improved so that by the time they were adults, they were able to create full-sized utilitarian objects.

Playing with dolls and other toys also created opportunities for children to interact with each other and increased their socialization skills. Reenacting ceremonies with dolls taught children about tribal traditions. Miniature cradle boards and dolls, tipis, and bows and arrows also allowed children to practice grown-up activities, with boys focusing on hunting and war and girls on domestic skills.

---

spend a maximum of twenty minutes in an exhibit, the more succinct a label's message, the more quickly it is delivered, and the more likely the visitor is to absorb it. (See textbox 4.3 for a sample case label with a headline as its first sentence.) Additional information on writing labels can be found in textbox 4.4 and *Exhibit Labels: An Interpretive Approach* (see the resource section at the end of this chapter).

Design

The primary goal of exhibit graphic design is to make the written message legible and accessible. The typeface needs to be easy to read with letters at least one-quarter inch high and considerably larger if the label is to be understood from any distance. (Letter height varies depending on the font, but one-quarter inch is equivalent to a font size of at least eighteen points.) A background color with a high contrast to the type color works best. Many techniques that seem elegant or creative actually result in text that is difficult to read if they are used for more than one sentence. This includes reverse type (light color on dark background), centered or justified (as opposed to flush-left) text, and accents like italics, underlining, and boldface. Lettering on clear acrylic with no background can also be difficult to read or, if poorly lit, may cast shadows on the objects or even on the other lines of text. Even if the wall or case interior is covered with

---

TEXTBOX 4.4

TOP FOUR LABEL-WRITING TIPS

Number 4: Keep it short—75 words maximum per paragraph and 150 words maximum per label. One-third shorter is even better, especially for heavily interactive exhibits or those aimed at a younger audience. The tight limit not only increases readership but also helps to keep the focus on your message.

Number 3: Avoid jargon and eliminate fancy words. We are here to communicate, not to show off our vocabularies.

Number 2: Go through the label, and try to change any inactive verbs—is, are, was, were, been, become, has, have, and so forth. Describe the objects and characters as *doing* something rather than sitting around just *being* something. Avoid the passive voice. Instead of saying, "The fossil was buried by a flooding river," write, "A flooding river buried the fossil." (Active voice has the added advantage of almost always being a couple of words shorter.)

But the number 1 piece of advice is this: After each draft, read the label aloud to discover whether it flows well and makes sense. If the person who wrote the label trips over the language, visitors reading it cold for the first time, or reading it to their kids, are guaranteed to have problems.

---

a pattern, the label background should always be solid. An exhibit of Ghanaian pottery at the Art Institute of Chicago made good use of an exuberant, geometric, African-inspired wall covering, but printing the labels on the same pattern made them almost impossible to decipher.

Various publications and websites provide detailed information about compliance with Americans with Disabilities Act (ADA) requirements for graphics. Additional guidelines can be found in *Standards Manual for Signs and Labels* (see the resource section).

Exhibit and Case Layout

Good exhibit design makes the most of the unique characteristics of a museum identified in table 4.1. Key factors include clear organization and thoughtful utilization of the three-dimensional nature of the space.

Of primary importance is an easy-to-follow story line with each case or component telling a self-contained part of the whole narrative. This allows visitors to take different paths through the exhibit space without confusion. Take into account multiple entrances to the exhibit space as well as any routes visitors generally use. If visitors typically follow one path from one room to another, sequential parts of the exhibit can be laid out along that path. If the exhibit requires a set path, signage or labels can be used to make it clear; visitors should never feel like they have entered at the middle or end of an exhibit.

Try to use the space so that visitors are surrounded by and immersed in the exhibit. Rather than placing cases or components around the perimeter of the room, wherever possible create a path that allows visitors to walk between them. Not all three-dimensional objects need be in cases; some can be displayed on the walls on foam core or other solid backing, protected by an acrylic box or frame. Good exhibit design also needs to comply with ADA requirements, allowing space for wheelchair accessibility and providing clear sight lines for the visually impaired.

The color of the room can set the tone of an exhibit. Bright primary colors create very different effects than light pastels or deep, dramatic shades. Cases painted to blend in with the floor or walls can make a small space look bigger. Walls painted in warm colors (reds and yellows) make rooms seem smaller; cool colors (blues and greens) make them seem bigger.

Individual case layouts should also take advantage of the three-dimensional nature of the space, setting groups of objects at various heights and depths. Evenly spaced objects on a shelf or wall may keep the visitors' attention if the individual items have intrinsic dimensionality and variety, like mineral specimens. However, visitors will quickly lose interest in regular rows of objects of the same size and shape, like stone tools or photographic images. Layouts should strive

Photo 4.4. Balanced asymmetry. The two halves of this case are not mirror images, yet each side carries the same visual "weight": the three tall vases on the left are balanced by the numerous smaller pieces on the right, with the plate in the center as an anchoring fulcrum. Notice, too, how the designer used the depth of the case, and even added plinths to vary the height of objects, adding visual dynamism. (Courtesy of Eugene Dillenburg)

for "balanced asymmetry," with a large object on one side of the case balanced by several small objects on the other or a large object on a tall pedestal surrounded by smaller objects mounted closer to the base. The asymmetry creates a sense of dynamism and movement, while the balance maintains a sense of order. (See photo 4.4 for an example.)

Different pieces of information can be contained in a single case by grouping closely related items together and using the spaces between the groups to create a visual separation. Alternatively, placing a single object alone in a case draws attention to the object and emphasizes its importance. Focusing on a particularly important, large, or dramatic object, especially at the beginning of an exhibit or in a place easily visible from the entrance, serves to draw visitors into the space. For museums with a large school and family audience, it is important to remember that objects above a certain height will be invisible to many children.

In general, the "less is more" rule works well in museum exhibits. Exhibits should communicate, not overwhelm. A single well-chosen example can be much more effective and engaging that a dozen nearly identical items. A well-laid-out case leaves space between objects and allows each to shine. Space can also change the visitors' perception of a particular type of object. For example, exhibiting quilts fully opened and spaced out on the walls reinforces their aesthetic value as individual art objects, whereas displaying them folded emphasizes their more familiar role as utilitarian household items.

There are times, however, when a more crowded case can also make a point, such as abundance or diversity. For example, the Northwest Coast gallery at the Field Museum is particularly dense with objects and photographs. While it is the norm for museums of this size and scope to display only 1 to 2 percent of their collections in a given area, the Field Museum has almost 75 percent of its Northwest Coast collection on display. Despite some criticisms that this is overkill, the approach provides a very direct experience of the richness not only of the museum's collection but also of the culture itself.

Within individual cases, the choice of a contrasting background color not only makes the objects more visible but can also support part of the exhibit message. For example, mounting Southwestern Indian silver and turquoise jewelry on purple velvet makes a connection with the clothing that Navajo women traditionally wear with these pieces. Using a different color or fabric for case interiors and mounts in each gallery or part of an exhibit provides a recognizable "signature" for the different spaces. Appropriately patterned fabric can also provide geographic or cultural cues, like a grassy green fabric used in a Great Plains exhibit or a pale blue and white background for Arctic carvings. Of course, it is important for the pattern or background not to overwhelm objects. Finally, for organic materials that are subject to pest infestation, a solid, light-colored background makes it easier to see any insect frass (excrement) or other debris.

In smaller museums with limited time, manpower, and money, it is often impractical to draw detailed layouts of case interiors. However, for particularly complex cases, laying out the exhibit materials on a flat surface the same size and shape as the case allows for experimentation with different layouts. A floor plan showing the location of cases and components and identifying the interpretive materials ensures that everything fits and that no sections get lost. Computer programs like Floorplanner (www.floorplanner.com) and Google Sketchup (http://sketchup.google.com) can assist with creating both two- and three-dimensional designs.

Mounting the Exhibit

At installation time the content and design decisions are tested against the physical reality of the exhibit space. Items may be added or removed, object selection altered, and changes made in how topics are presented. For example, it may make more sense either for space or content purposes to use a photograph instead of an object. In small museums, which often have less time for exhibit development or design, space or time restrictions may require that sections of the exhibit be reorganized or condensed. Of course, major changes in the size or number of cases or mounts may be costly and time-consuming, so it is important to plan as carefully as possible. With any revision, the ultimate goal remains to present the main message clearly using the available resources of time, money, and manpower.

Most importantly, when exhibiting original objects, be they two- or three-dimensional, make sure they are protected from damage due either to handling by visitors, environmental factors, or the exhibit process itself. (See textbox 4.5 for specific conservation guidelines for exhibits.) Mounts should never be attached directly to objects with any kind of hardware or adhesive.

The method for limiting visitors' access to objects on display will vary depending on the exhibit layout, the nature of the museum, and the type of visitor. For museums with many children and family visitors, cases and frames are the preferable means for protecting original objects. Historic houses or museums with a large number of docents, interpreters, or gallery attendants may rely on ropes or other barrier systems. Of course, exceptions can be made when there is a compelling reason. For example, at the Mitchell Museum of the American Indian, a large number of the visitors are families and children on school tours. Although most objects are displayed inside closed cases, for interpretative reasons it was decided to show a full-sized canoe in the open almost at ground level, "protected" by the volunteer at the front desk. Touching restrictions were explained to visitors at entry. Often the younger visitors paid attention while their parents needed to be reminded, "Dad, the lady said not to touch the canoe!"

Smaller museums generally do not have the resources to create custom cases for each new exhibit but reuse exhibit furniture and materials from one exhibit to another. When there are funds for new case construction, often through grants or special donations, it is best for the case design to be as versatile as possible, perhaps providing vitrines (acrylic lids) of different heights for similar-sized wooden bases. The more specialized the case, the less likely that it can be reused. *Help! For the Small Museum* includes detailed instructions on building simple cases (see the resource list).

Larger museums may be willing to donate unwanted exhibit furniture from their past temporary exhibits. Other recycled cases may come from local stores. If necessary, simple modifications can be made, like building wooden platforms to raise the height of the case or adding wheels to make it more mobile. (See photo 4.5)

The physical exhibit space itself may pose installation challenges. Doors, windows, and even construction materials may require creative solutions. Holes

Photo 4.5. A base and wheels were added to a donated department store jewelry display case. (Courtesy of Putnam County Museum, Inc., Greencastle, Indiana)

drilled in brick or concrete walls to hang objects are permanent and should only be made after careful thought. Any change in exhibit design may leave the holes as an ugly distraction. Mounting objects directly on walls with painted, paneled, or other finished surfaces may also leave scars that will need to be covered or fixed in the future. Alternatives to drilling into these types of walls include hanging the objects from a wooden railing permanently affixed to the walls or from hooks screwed into the ceiling. The size or layout of the exhibit space can also be modified through simple techniques like building temporary walls from doors hinged together or closing off areas using curtains hung from inexpensive rods.

Appropriate materials and installation techniques for mounts, cases, and frames provide protection and stability for objects and ensure that they do not chemically react with any of the mounting materials. A list of acceptable and unacceptable materials for case construction is listed in table 4.3.

A wide variety of chemically inert plastic mounts, mini easels, risers, and other display items are available commercially. Object mounts can also be made in-house using relatively inexpensive materials. Blocks of inert foam or wood, painted to match the cases or covered with appropriate fabric, can be used to create multilevel platforms.

Objects can be displayed on a slant by tying them to sheets of fabric-covered foam core or heavy cardboard with monofilament (nylon fishing line, commonly sold in hardware stores). Monofilament can also be used to stabilize objects on their mounts, while nails covered with inert plastic tubing can prevent objects from moving inside the case.

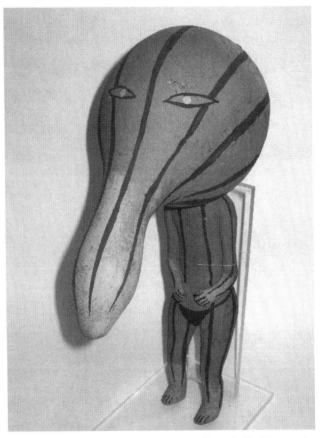

Photo 4.6. Monofilament holds the Squash Kachina to its acrylic base. (Courtesy of Janice Klein)

Table 4.3. Case Construction

Acceptable	Unacceptable
Case Construction Materials	
Acid-free paper and board	Carpeting
Acrylic adhesive and paints	Drying oil paints
Ceramics	Formaldehyde-containing products
Cotton (undyed)	Formica
Glass	Lead-based paints
Linen (undyed)	Oil-based paints
Metals	Poly-sulphide adhesives
Plexiglas	Polyurethane resins and foams
Polyester fabrics (Dacron, Terylene)	Polyvinyl acetate emulsified resins
Polyester sheeting (Mylar Type D)	Polyvinyl acetate latex-based paints
Polyethylene foam (Ethafoam)	Polyvinyl chloride
Polyethylene plastic sheeting	Rubber derivatives
Sealed woods (see below for woods and sealants)	Sulphur dyes
	Unsealed wood
	Vulcanized rubber
	Wood pulp paper products
	Wool
Wood	
Balsa	Butternut
Birch	Cypress
Exterior Plywood	Douglas fir
Maple	Hickory
Marine Plywood	Oak
Particleboard made without formaldehyde resin	Particleboard/chipboard
(i.e., Medex, Medite II, Resincore I)	Pecan
Poplar	Pressed-fiber board (Homosote)
	Red cedar
	Redwood
	Southern yellow pine
	Sweet chestnut
Wood Sealants	
Acrylic paints (two to three coats)	Alkyd-based paints
Latex urethane acrylic (Benjamin Moore #416)	Lead-based paints
Marvelseal (aluminum/polyethylene foil)	Oil-based paints
Moisture-cured urethanes (non-oil modified)	Oil-modified polyurethanes
Shellac (two to three coats)	Polyvinyl acetate latex paints
Two-part epoxy paints	
Gasketing	
Acrylic felt	Rubber
Brush nylon	Rubber derivatives
Barrier Materials	
Acid-free paper, board, or tissue	Carpeting
Linen (washed and undyed)	Polyurethane foams
Melinex (Type 456 or 516)	Silk
Muslin (washed and undyed)	Wool
Mylar Type D	
Plexiglas	
Polyester fabric	
Tyvek	

*Based on recommendations of Catherine Sease, fellow of the American Institute for Conservation

Photo 4.7. Beadwork is mounted inside the modified cardboard box of the acrylic frame. (Courtesy of Janice Klein)

Mini cases for objects with a relatively low profile, like textiles or beadwork, can be made out of plastic box frames by cutting one side off of the cardboard insert provided with the frame. The cardboard can be covered with fabric or another inert material, the object tied to the covered cardboard using monofilament, and the insert slid back into the plastic frame. (See photo 4.7.)

Textiles can be hung by hand-sewing a fabric sleeve made of polyester bias tape or hem facing onto the rear top edge of the textile. A wooden dowel or curtain rod covered with acid-free tissue or lay-flat plastic tubing is inserted through the sleeve. (See photo 4.8.) Monofilament threaded through eye hooks at the end of the dowel allows it to hang from the wall or ceiling using cup hooks or curtain rod brackets. Three-dimensional objects can also be hung using slings of monofilament covered with plastic tubing.

Original two-dimensional materials, like photographs, letters, and other archival materials, require the same care and protection as three-dimensional objects. Displaying them in frames or inside cases is the optimum choice, but in no event should holes be created using any kind of tack or pin. Similarly, original objects should never be attached by glue or other adhesive to a backing or wall.

Display boards made of foam core covered with fabric, similar to those described above, can also be used for two-dimensional objects. Instead of tying the object to the backing, it can be secured using T-pins placed above and below to hold it in place. (See photo 4.9.)

Alternatively, many two-dimensional materials can be easily reproduced by scanning. They can be made any size, using a commercial photocopier. Depending on the overall replacement cost, many of these reproductions can be mounted directly on gallery walls.

Photo 4.8. The textile is hung by a curtain rod inserted through the cloth sleeve. (Courtesy of Janice Klein)

Photo 4.9. Quilt squares are held on fabric-covered foam core by T-pins. (Courtesy of the Montgomery County Cultural Foundation)

There are many techniques for creating and mounting labels, ranging from paper labels to professionally designed and produced banners. While computer-generated paper labels do not have a particularly long life, they are easily replaced and revised. Most word processors come with a wide variety of font faces and sizes. The label can be dry-mounted (a process that uses heat and pressure to adhere paper onto foam core board), glued onto cardstock, backed with colored paper, or framed. If placed inside the case, labels can be laid flat, tented, or placed in acrylic sign holders; outside the case, they can be taped to the wall or side of the case with Scotch Wall Mounting Tabs or mounted in frames.

Remember These Five Guidelines

1. The museum exhibit is a medium for communication with special characteristics. Make the best use possible of those characteristics. Visitor research examines how people behave in museums; whenever possible, make use of those findings.
2. Every exhibit tells a story, but just one story. Not every aspect of a story will fit in the exhibit. There will be more exhibits to tell more stories.
3. Very little in exhibit construction needs to be expensive: reuse, recycle, and rethink. Spend money and time in creating cases and mounts that can be used repeatedly and in different combinations. Ultimately, creativity is more important than money.
4. Do not forget the museum's mission to care for its collection in developing and designing the exhibit. Collection objects on display need special protection.
5. Ideally, an exhibit will be both educational and enjoyable for the visitor. Do not sacrifice one for the other; both are equally important.

EXHIBIT CONSERVATION GUIDELINES

These guidelines are based on the recommendations of Catherine Sease, fellow, American Institute for Conservation. See chapter 1 in Book 6 of this series for more explanation of the causes of deterioration and preservation of collections.

Environment
1. Temperature and relative humidity levels should remain as constant as possible, within a range of 60°F to 75°F and 40–55 percent relative humidity. Heating and cooling systems should not be turned off in the exhibit spaces at night.
2. There should be no natural light in exhibit areas. All windows and skylights should be covered by shades or blinds. Fluorescent lights should be covered by ultraviolet (UV) filters (UF3 or equivalent). Maximum acceptable UV radiation on organic materials is seventy-five microwatts per lumen. Incandescent lights should be mounted outside of cases, at a sufficient distance to avoid overheating the objects. If the surface of an object feels warm, the light is too close.
3. Acceptable light levels:
   - 5 fc (50 lux) for sensitive organic materials, including textiles, dyed leather, paper, feathers, fur, and basketry
   - 15 fc (150 lux) for other organic materials, including wood, undyed leather, bone, ivory, horn, animal skin or hide, and paintings
   - unrestricted for nonorganic materials, including metal, unpainted stone, unpainted ceramics, and glass

Cases
1. Freestanding cases should be adequately weighted with sandbags or affixed to the floor to prevent them from moving when bumped.
2. Exhibit cases and other materials in the case (props) should be constructed of materials that are free of acids and emit the least possible amount of volatile chemicals. All raw wood surfaces should be sealed with paint or polyurethane. All case interiors should be allowed to off-gas (dry in open air) for at least one week, and preferably three weeks, prior to object installation. (See table 4.3 in this chapter for more information.)

(continued)

TEXTBOX 4.5 (*Continued*)

3. Objects should not be placed in direct contact with wood surfaces, even when they have been sealed. All materials that come in direct contact with the object should be stable. A piece of acid-free paper or thin plastic (e.g., Mylar) can be placed under the object to provide a barrier between the object and any non-acid-free material. Plexiglas, plastic tubing and bags, and muslin, linen, and polyester fabric are also acceptable.
4. No organic material (e.g., wood, leaves) should be placed in the same case as an object.

Mounts
1. Mounts should adequately support the weight of the object and hold it securely without subjecting it to excessive strain.
2. Mounts should never be permanently attached to an object. No wax, adhesive, or pressure-sensitive tape (e.g., double-sided tape) should be used to hold objects in place. Objects should never be tacked, nailed, or stapled to a board, backing, or wall.
3. Clamps and brackets should be padded with nonabrasive, inert material (e.g., plastic tubing, nonwool felt, or moleskin).
4. Objects should not be placed in contact with one another or touch any part of the plastic or glass of a vitrine. To prevent uneven fading, no portion of an object should be covered by another object or any other material.
5. Objects should not be hung by any of their parts, such as handles, loops, or drawstrings, no matter what their original purpose. Objects made of textiles, paper, or barkcloth should not be mounted with sharp folds or pleats.

Resources

American Association of Museums (AAM). *Standards Manual for Signs and Labels.* Washington, DC: AAM, 1995.

Borowsky, Larry. *Telling a Story in 100 Words: Effective Label Copy.* American Association for State and Local History (AASLH) Technical Leaflet 240. Nashville, TN: AASLH, 2007.

Doe, Paula C., Curtis A. Peacock, and R. Eli Paul. *Exhibition Mounts on a Budget.* American Association for State and Local History (AASLH) Technical Leaflet 187. Nashville, TN: AASLH, 1993.

Falk, John H., and Lynn D. Dierking. *Learning from Museums: Visitor Experiences and the Making of Museums*. Lanham, MD: AltaMira Press, 2000.

———. *The Museum Experience*. Washington, DC: Whalesback Books, 1992.

Hein, George E. *Learning in the Museum*. Florence, KY: Routledge, 1998.

Kennedy, Jeff. *User Friendly: Hands-On Exhibits That Work*. Washington, DC: Association of Science-Technology Centers, 1990.

Kenney, Kimberly. "How to Create an Exhibit on a Shoestring Budget." BellaOnline. 2006. www.bellaonline.com/articles/art41973.asp.

McLean, Kathleen. *Planning for People in Museum Exhibits*. Washington, DC: Association of Science-Technology Centers, 1993.

Miles, R. S. *The Design of Educational Exhibits*. Florence, KY: Routledge, 1988.

National Endowment for the Arts and National Endowment for the Humanities. *Design for Accessibility: A Cultural Administrator's Handbook*. Washington, DC: National Association of State Arts Agencies, 2003.

Neal, Aminta. *Help! For the Small Museum. Handbook of Exhibit Ideas and Methods*. Boulder, CO: Pruett Press, 1969.

Orselli, Paul, ed. *Cheapbook: A Compendium of Inexpensive Exhibit Ideas*. Washington, DC: Association of Science-Technology Centers, 1995.

———, ed. *Cheapbook 2: A Compendium of Inexpensive Exhibit Ideas*. Washington, DC: Association of Science-Technology Centers, 1999.

———, ed. *Cheapbook 3: A Compendium of Inexpensive Exhibit Ideas*. Washington, DC: Association of Science-Technology Centers, 2004.

Parman, Alice, and Jeffrey Jane Flowers. *Exhibit Makeovers: A Do-It-Yourself Workbook for Small Museums*. Lanham, MD: AltaMira Press, 2008.

Salmen, John P. S., ed. *Everyone's Welcome*. Washington, DC: American Association of Museums 1998.

Serrell, Beverly. *Exhibit Labels: An Interpretative Approach*. Lanham, MD: AltaMira Press, 1996.

Smithsonian Institution. *Smithsonian Guidelines for Accessible Exhibition Design*. Washington, DC: Smithsonian Institution Press, 2000.

Taylor, Samuel. *Try It: Improving Exhibits through Formative Evaluation*. Washington, DC: Association of Science-Technology Centers, 1991.

Note

1. The words "exhibition" and "exhibit" are sometimes given different, specific meanings and refer variously to a gallery, a hall, a large installation, or a small display within that larger context (i.e., an individual case, display, or interactive station). "Exhibit" will be used here to include all those meanings.

THE NUTS AND BOLTS OF PROGRAM MANAGEMENT

Rebecca Martin

Much of the world knows our museums through our programs. Community members and tourists plan to attend festivals and other outdoor events or find themselves drawn in as they pass by; school children encounter us in their classrooms and on field trips; young professionals fill their social calendars by participating in our evening events.

Therefore, our programs are powerful tools. They let our communities know that we exist, they develop new audiences, and they create a public face for our institutions. And, of course, they are one of our most visible means to advance our mission. There are many reasons to create programs (which, I would argue, are essential to the success of most small museums). But no matter how important the reason for holding it, a poorly conceived or executed workshop, school field trip, concert, symposium, or festival does not benefit the organization. Instead, it drains resources and damages an institution's reputation.

The good news is that you can do much to ensure the success of your programming. Start by making sure you understand your museum's purpose. While it might be tempting to dive into planning an event or a school visit, program development and management should not happen until you have a clear sense of who you are and what you are trying to accomplish. Has your institution grappled with delineating its purpose? Do you have a well-defined mission that is understood by all staff and board members? A well-developed mission statement and a commitment on the part of the staff and the board to adhere to it are preliminary requirements for all museum activities. (If your institution's mission is vague or irrelevant to the current direction of the organization, see chapter 3 in Book 1 of this series.) Effective organizations—those that work to achieve their missions—align all their activities to it. The American Association for State and Local History standards for mission, vision, and governance remind us that museums should ensure that "all aspects of the institution's operations are integrated and focused on meeting its mission." In practical terms, this concept means that you decide which programs you will run based on whether they will help you achieve your institution's goals.

Next, planning will ensure that you design and implement effective programs. Some large institutions formalize the process for proposing and approving activities. The Senator John Heinz History Center, in Pittsburgh, Pennsylvania, for example, offers a model that small organizations can use to help them determine the feasibility of an idea. Before committing fully to a program, jot down some preliminary thoughts. You might want to consider the questions below, adapted from a form that the Senator John Heinz History Center uses, to help assess every potential exhibition. The questions range from content to logistics.

- How would you describe the program?
- How does the program support the mission of the organization?
- Which key audience segment will the topic appeal to?
- What is the time frame for the program?
- What is the proposed cost for the program?
- Are collections available to support the program?

Roughing out the idea for a program will help you decide whether you want to invest resources—including your time—in developing it.

TEXTBOX 5.1

MISSION AND PROGRAMS

Imagine that you are a local historical society from a largely agricultural community with a collection of objects and manuscripts that date mainly from the late nineteenth and early twentieth centuries, and you would like to build your visitation among upper elementary school students. A stakeholder suggests that since novels about magic are pretty popular with young people right now, a wizard-themed sleepover program might attract a big audience. Let your mission help you decide whether this program is a good fit. Perhaps you like the sleepover idea, but you decide that the topic suggested does not match your mission. Think about other themes that might work better. For instance, baseball was a popular sport in many rural communities during the late nineteenth and early twentieth centuries. Take a look at your collection to see whether you have any baseball-related items or descriptions of ball games. Consider developing a program that helps your young visitors connect their lives to the lives of people in the past by playing baseball according to period rules and celebrating the victors with refreshments typical of the era.

Once you have decided to go ahead with a program idea, you will need to start planning in earnest. In fact, the majority of the work of a program is done before the event begins. This workflow is concretely represented by the allotment of space in this chapter. Just as three-quarters of the chapter's pages focus on the planning process, three-quarters of the time you devote to any program will be spent on planning. The sections below outline the different kinds of work that you will need to do to prepare for your event. You may do them in the order in which they appear, or you may go through them in a different sequence. You will likely find yourself going through some of these steps simultaneously. In all program planning, remember to draw upon your experience creating or attending other programs. If you have ever held or participated in a program, you already know a lot about what works well and what does not.

Planning

Who Is the Audience?

No program can serve every imaginable participant. For example, the presentation style that makes the most sense for elementary school students is likely not the one best suited for high schoolers. And although program content might interest both retirees and parents of small children, the two groups have different scheduling needs.

Think about what programs your museum has offered over the years and which have been especially successful. Reflect on the makeup of your membership. Do retired adults, families with young school-age children, longtime residents, or newcomers comprise the majority of your members? Sometimes the best strategy is to develop programs for well-established audiences. For example, the Museum of Vision, operated by the Foundation of the American Academy of Ophthalmology in San Francisco, focuses most of its programming on its core constituency of ophthalmologists—both working physicians and physicians in training. In order to meet the needs of this main audience group, the museum plans symposia and lectures that are full of technical detail and therefore too difficult for most other visitors. The museum has decided that it makes the best use of its resources by focusing its programming on one audience.

In other instances, programs can help introduce the museum to new visitors. The Litchfield Historical Society of Litchfield, Connecticut, for example, has worked with the local parks and recreation office to offer weekly activities for its summer camp program. This arrangement broadens the organization's reach to include many preschool- and school-age children whose families are not regular museum visitors. Serving these visitors may also pay later dividends. Some of these children return to the society's two museums with their parents. And as these young people grow and gain more exposure to the organization through

Photo 5.1. Families with young children are enjoying an outdoor concert of late eighteenth- and early nineteenth-century music. (Courtesy of the Litchfield Historical Society, Litchfield, Connecticut)

other extracurricular programs and field trips, some of them become long-term supporters of the society.

Remember, however, to be thoughtful about what new audiences are appropriate for your institution. The Litchfield Historical Society has very few visitors who are young professionals without children. Although some museums have built strong constituencies from this population, the Litchfield Historical Society has made the decision not to focus its programming efforts on this demographic, as there are very few childless professionals in their twenties and early thirties in Litchfield, a small town of eight thousand located about an hour's drive from Hartford. The organization makes more effective use of its resources by concentrating on other segments of the population.

You know your museum's community best, but some of the audiences you might consider targeting for a specific program are

- retirees;
- families with young children;
- high school students;
- professionals looking for an activity during a lunch break;
- adults with an interest in your content area;
- young professionals;
- people with ancestral connections to community.

Sometimes you may want to be even more specific about the audience segment you would like to reach through your program. For example, if your community has had an influx of immigrants from a particular part of the world, and you have not yet seen much visitation from members of this community, you might want to design a program that will help these new residents learn about and feel welcome at your site. You might also want to consider the effect that gender has on your program participation. For instance, you might discover that your classes on nineteenth-century stenciling techniques draw in more women than men and try to balance the appeal of your programs by offering a course on a topic that is more traditionally associated with men, such as historical furniture-construction techniques.

If your museum has other staff, make sure that everyone understands what group you are trying to reach with this particular program. In some organizations, where board members fill unpaid staff as well as governance functions, key board members will also need to be part of discussions about a program's intended audience.

Once you have settled on the target group, you will want to start thinking about the requirements of whichever group is your focus. If you are planning a mid-morning gallery talk aimed at senior citizens, for example, remember that some seniors have difficulty standing for long periods. Consider whether you will ask the participants to be on their feet for the entire program. Could you instead place seating throughout the exhibition space? Or could you structure the program so that participants look briefly at a few items on exhibit and then gather in a comfortable sitting area to learn about the objects they have just viewed? Perhaps the program could end with another brief visit to the gallery.

Events for young professionals should have their own characteristics. Programs scheduled after work or on Saturday evenings can appeal to young, active people who are looking for social events. People in this demographic often search for opportunities to meet new people and to socialize with those they know already. If you are a local history museum, perhaps you might build on your traditional celebration of local artists by holding an open mike night for aspiring area artists to perform their material. You might design an evening event as a team-based scavenger hunt. Invite potential participants to form themselves into teams and to register for the event. Suggest that each group select a name and offer a prize for the team that wins the competition.

Programs intended for young children need to be shorter in duration than those for older children. Often, preschool children and students in the primary grades have more fun and can focus better when a program includes a variety of activities. Check your museum's bookshelf for *The Docent Educator*'s basic overview of child development (Alan Gartenhaus and Jackie Littleton, eds., *The Best of the Docent Educator: A Comprehensive Manual for Those Who Teach with*

Institutional Collections [Kamuela, HI : The Docent Educator, 1998], 49–53). Your local library or a quick Web search should yield other references on child development. You might consider reading through the national standards for history (available at the National Center for History in the School's website, www.sscnet.ucla.edu/nchs/standards) to get a sense of what knowledge of history students are likely to have in what grade. This reference also provides information on the historical thinking abilities of children of different ages.

When planning programs for school groups, think about not only the school curriculum and how your program fits into it but also the school schedule. Do classes in your area begin at 7:30 a.m.? 8 a.m.? 8:30 a.m.? Do students of different ages have different beginning and ending times? What time is dismissal? How many minutes before dismissal must students be back in the building at the end of a field trip? Schools are often constrained by the cost of field trips. If you are interested in attracting school groups, you might want to investigate whether any donors or area foundations are willing to help underwrite the cost of busing students to your site. (See textbox 5.2 for more information on working with school groups.)

Sometimes events or trends in your community will cause you to think about serving a new audience. Staff at Gadsby's Tavern Museum in Alexandria, Virginia, for instance, noticed an increase in the number of mothers walking through town with toddlers and saw that, during the day, coffee shops and public spaces near their museum were full of these potential visitors. Once they recognized this possible new audience, the staff realized it had an opportunity to expand the way it was meeting its educational mission of "creat[ing] a varied and meaningful learning environment that addresses the needs and interests of the community's residents and visitors" (http://oha.alexandriava.gov/gadsby/gt-mission.html). Accordingly, the staff responded to the new situation by developing a monthly program called Tavern Toddlers. This one-and-a-half-hour program includes a craft and a story. Each month, the program features a different theme related to the historic site and its surroundings. Staff kept the needs of young children and caregivers in mind when they developed the program. Each session features a variety of age-appropriate activities designed to suit the short attention span of toddlers. The program also provides the adults who attend with time to socialize with each other. The program is scheduled for mid-morning, avoiding the after-lunch nap time of most young children. Tavern Toddlers is a good fit for Gadsby's Tavern Museum because it has a strong mission connection and enables the institution to further its goal of being a center of community life.

What Do You Hope to Achieve through This Program?

After answering the fundamental questions of how the program will advance the mission and who the audience is, move on to other considerations. Most

PROGRAMS FOR SCHOOL GROUPS

For many institutions, school groups have long been a natural and important audience. For many years, schools have built regular field trips into their schedules. Historic sites are often eager to accommodate school groups, as they value sharing their knowledge with young people. Although many schools today have limited or eliminated field trips for students, this audience remains an important one. Schools face many challenges related to field trips, however, and you can take some steps to make them more viable for teachers. First, make sure—through your publicity materials or individual conversations—that you show teachers how your content connects to the material they teach. Second, remember that many schools are facing severe budget constraints, so low fees can make a difference. You might consider offering to take your program to the school if it does not seem feasible for the students to visit your site.

You will be most successful at developing a school audience if you begin by looking closely at your mission and your state's curriculum standards to determine where the two intersect. Standards are arranged by grade level and by subject. And while national standards exist, each state has its own set. To find your state's curriculum standards (sometimes called a "framework"), go to the website of your state's department of education. While you might be really excited to teach seventh graders about the history of rice cultivation in your community, you will likely run into difficulty convincing teachers to participate in a school program on the subject if the seventh-grade curriculum is about ancient Egypt, Greece, and Rome. Instead, think about what you can offer that will help teachers accomplish their goals. If your site is situated in Nebraska and explores the pioneer experience, you will want to learn which grades study westward expansion. Then, by reading carefully the standards related to the subject, you can craft a program that meets some of the curricular goals for those grades.

Next, decide whether you would like to develop a close relationship with your local schools and develop your programming to fit tightly with their needs or whether you prefer to create a menu of programs and publicize them equally to all area schools. Consider whether you see your school programming as a public service that your organization is willing to underwrite, as an activity that needs to pay for itself, or as a way to earn income to support other areas of operation. If you need to charge schools to participate but fear that fees will be a barrier to their attendance, consider looking for a local business or foundation to sponsor their participation in your programs.

Finally, when planning school programs, think carefully about scheduling and logistics. Schools are rigid in their starting and ending times. Buses are often available for only limited periods. Make sure that you offer your programs at a time that will suit your audience. Many groups will be able to leave school only after the buses are finished delivering students to the building. They will need to have students back in time for dismissal and for the buses to move into their places to collect students for the ride home. If you plan to host a school group for the entire day, think about lunch options. Do you have a place for the students to eat? Is there a place for teachers to store coolers if they have carried lunches in them? How many chaperones do you require for the students? Is there a limit to the number of adults that you can accommodate with the program? Make sure you have communicated all of these details to the coordinating teacher so that the group leaders will know what to expect. Send a confirmation outlining any fees you will charge, the time you expect the group, the duration of the planned activity, the location where the group should meet you, and how many people you expect will be in the group. Do not forget to include your contact information.

Home-school groups may want to participate in your programs. These groups often include students at different levels. You might have toddlers through teenagers. Decide ahead of time whether the program will work with a vast difference in ages.

Some teachers may want suggestions for ways to prepare their students for the visit. Consider developing some activities that teachers can do in the classroom to tie the trip to the students' regular schoolwork. As with other kinds of museum programming, planning can make the difference between a successful or disappointing school visit.

institutions have several goals for holding a particular program. As you develop a new program or begin the planning process for a program you have offered in the past, identify your primary purpose in sponsoring the activity. Knowing why you are holding the program will help you with other decisions, including how to fund, market, and evaluate the event. Make sure that you are also clear about any additional goals. For example, your primary or secondary purpose for the activity might be to

- teach a concept;
- inculcate a skill;
- attract a new audience;
- earn income;

- raise the profile of the institution;
- develop relationships with other organizations;
- be a good neighbor;
- promote an exhibition;
- provide entertainment.

The relative importance of each goal may change according to the program. However, every program should include a goal of increasing your audience's understanding of content related to your institution.

The President Benjamin Harrison Home in Indianapolis, Indiana, hosts a naturalization ceremony each summer. The program meets several of the organization's goals. With 80 to 110 individuals becoming citizens at each ceremony, the event introduces the museum to a large group of people as most of the petitioners, or prospective new citizens, attend the event with friends and family. The program helps the museum strengthen its connections with other organizations in the community: The local chapter of the Daughters of the American Revolution helps provide lemonade and cookies; the Indiana Bar Association sends representatives to the ceremony and gives a gift to each new citizen. By hosting the naturalization ceremony, the museum provides a service to the community. The program is an especially good fit for the museum, though, because it has a strong mission connection. Part of the President Benjamin Harrison Home's mission is "to increase public understanding of, appreciation for, and participation in the American system of self-government through the life stories of an American President." Helping people become citizens of the United States is an excellent way to "increase understanding of . . . and participation in the American system of self-government." And the program provides an opportunity for the museum to illuminate one of the important events of Harrison's administration: the opening of Ellis Island. Tours of the house and interactions with staff provide participants in the naturalization ceremony with opportunities to explore immigration and naturalization in the past and the present.

Another key element of developing programs is to make sure that you have well-defined learning goals for the participants. (See textbox 5.3.) In other words, what do you want visitors to be able to do or to understand as a result of participating in the program? How will you know if you have accomplished your objectives? For instance, one of the goals of a Litchfield Historical Society school program on political parties in the early republic is for students to leave able to articulate the differences between the views of the Federalists and the Democratic-Republicans. To assess whether students achieve this aim, the final activity of the program introduces the participants to late-eighteenth-century songs with political themes. Some of these songs joined new words to popular

SETTING EDUCATIONAL GOALS

There are many models to use for setting educational goals. One way is to ask yourself, "What should participants understand or be able to do as a result of attending this program?" If you cannot clearly articulate an answer to this question, you are not ready to move forward in your program planning.

Imagine that you are planning a program for elementary school students in the primary grades on letter writing. Your site interprets stories of early twentieth-century immigration to the United States. Your educational goals might be that participants understand (1) the elements of a letter (date, greeting, signature, address, return address, stamp, etc.) and (2) why letters were important to families separated by immigration.

If you are developing a workshop for adults on Danish food traditions that have been passed down through generations of descendents of immigrants, you might have a choice of educational goals. Perhaps your goal is for each visitor to learn both the recipe and technique for making the traditional round Danish pancakes called *ebelskiver*. Or you might not be concerned that participants know how to make the food; instead, your goal is that visitors gain an understanding of the way that food traditions have strengthened ethnic identity among Danish descendents. Deciding what you would like visitors to experience and learn will affect how you shape your program, so it is critical that you think through this piece early in your planning.

melodies. The students then work in groups to write new lyrics for melodies they know. The words must express the core beliefs of one of the early political parties. The extent to which students are able to articulate what they have learned provides one informal measure of the success of the program.

What Kind of Program Do You Want to Hold?

"Museum programming" is a catch-all phrase that encompasses many different kinds of activities. Common program types include hands-on craft or skills workshops, lectures, gallery talks, walking tours, exhibition tours, summer camps, full-day symposiums, demonstrations, activity stations, outdoor festivals, evening parties, and concerts.

Consider what format will best allow you to meet your goals. Imagine, for example, that your organization has a fine collection of floor cloths. You might want to bring attention to your holdings and help visitors appreciate the objects by offering a workshop on how to make these traditional floor coverings. You could arrange a slide lecture showing examples of historic floor cloths and picturing each step of the process of making them. But participants will probably better remember the steps and find the experience more satisfying if you present the material in a hands-on format and give them a chance to make their own floor cloths.

Be creative when thinking about your options. You might want to craft a program that uses the hands-on workshop format but are unable to manage the associated logistical issues. A lecture on floor cloth making would take far less time and require less space than an interactive workshop that resulted in a floor cloth for each person. The program might also cost less to present, as you would not need to purchase many (if any) materials. However, straight lectures are not particularly effective teaching methods. Consider offering the program in a demonstration format. Have the presenter make a floor cloth as the participants watch, allowing the visitors to see firsthand and touch the materials.

Programs that incorporate multiple speakers work as either a series with each session featuring a different person or a daylong event offering several sessions in succession. For instance, if you want to draw attention to your new exhibition on the suburbanization of your small town, you might have a three-part lecture series on associated topics. The talks could be spread out over a number of weeks or months. The first might examine land use in the community from settlement to the 1950s. The next could focus on the rise of tract housing in your town and elsewhere. A third talk might discuss the changes in the community that came about as a result of the influx of new people.

Be sure to think about your space as you mull over program formats—you will want to make sure that your program draws attention to your site without damaging it. Gadsby's Tavern Museum, for example, makes good use of its historic structure by holding dances in the historic ballroom. The museum offers period dancing lessons in the weeks leading up to each ball. Participants are encouraged—but not required—to wear period-appropriate clothing, and the refreshments reflect the kinds of food served at balls held at the tavern during the eighteenth and nineteenth centuries. These programs have an extremely strong mission connection, as they re-create events that actually happened in the space. What is more, they inflict minimal wear and tear on the rooms used. The ballroom was constructed to support dancing. By keeping the spaces free of collections objects, limiting the number of people who may participate in each event, and sticking to period-appropriate dances, Gadsby's Tavern Museum creates fun, educational programs that do not stress the historic structure.

You will want to think carefully about what activities are physically appropriate for your site. If your community was once an artists' colony, you might want to celebrate that history by sponsoring painting workshops. While land-scape painting sessions on your grounds might be an excellent idea, a still-life painting course in your galleries might damage your collections and facility. The next section helps you explore your options on those occasions when you determine that a program format is a good fit for your organization but might not be best held on your site itself.

Where Will You Hold the Program?

Once you have decided who the target audience is and what your goals are for the program, start thinking about how many people are likely to participate. Review attendance figures for similar programs that you have held in the past. If you are hosting a scholarly symposium and your museum has held such events in previous years, you may be able to predict fairly accurately the number of people who will register to attend. Remember, though, that attendance at every program depends on an array of variables. The topic, the speakers' reputations, the date of the program, the cost to participants, and the weather on the day of the event, to name a few, can all have a big impact on how many people choose to attend.

Having a sense of the size of the audience will help you decide where you should hold the program. Run through a mental venue checklist:

- How many people do you expect to attend?
- Will the program be held indoors or outdoors?
- If it will be held outdoors, will you need a tent or other kind of shelter?
- Will you need electricity, and will you have an adequate power source?
- Will the audience sit, stand, or move around for the program?
- If attendees will sit, do you have enough chairs?
- Will participants need table space to do any activities?
- Does the location need to be near public transportation?
- Does it have enough parking?
- Does the site meet accessibility requirements?
- If you intend to have food at the event, is there a place where it can be consumed?

Do you have an appropriate space at your own institution? If not, think about what other spaces in your community might work. Might another museum or nonprofit organization allow you to use its facilities or be interested in forming a partnership with you? Is there a local community center, school, or church hall that you might use? (See textbox 5.4 for more information on partnerships.)

Be sure to reflect on whether the program might damage your space. Craft activities, for example, can be a wonderful way to help visitors learn about the material culture and customs of the past. Before you launch a craft activity program, be sure that the space can handle any ensuing mess. Taping sheets of craft paper to tables or covering them with vinyl tablecloths can protect the surfaces of your program furniture. Think about the floor covering. Will the proposed activity damage the carpet, tile, wood, or linoleum? Some activities may never be appropriate inside your space. If you plan to teach children to make candles, for example, ask yourself whether you could live with hot wax spilled on your floors, walls, or program furniture. If not, take the program outside or devise another activity.

Similarly, always assess whether a proposed activity will affect collections objects. Perhaps you are considering showcasing your musical instrument collection during an evening concert program for young professionals. Is the condition of the objects good enough to allow exhibition? Does the program area have space for cases to hold the instruments? If you are planning to have dancing, is there a place to situate the cases so that they are protected from jostling? Featuring collections in programming is an excellent way to link the activity to the educational part of the mission. But be sure that the program does not jeopardize your museum's preservation responsibilities.

What Is Your Schedule?

To make sure that you are on track to get everything done in a timely fashion, create a planning and event schedule. Start with the program itself and work backwards, thinking about all the steps that you need to accomplish in order to hold the event. For example, if you need people to register for the program, when will the response deadline be? Then ask yourself how much notice potential participants need before they must respond, and you will know when you need to send an e-mail announcement, mail invitations, and post flyers. How much time will it take to assemble the mailing once you get the materials from the printer? Next, find out how much time the printer needs in order to have the job to you by that date. Will it take you a week to design the invitation? Then you need to have all the final details about the participant fee, date, time, and location of the event by one week before the file must be at the printer. Mark all these dates on a calendar, and you will start to develop a time line of what must be done by when. Do not forget to make sure that everyone who is involved in the program planning understands the schedule.

A NOTE ABOUT PARTNERSHIPS

Working with other institutions can offer tremendous benefits. Partnerships can also create challenges. Sometimes organizations choose simply to cooperate with each other; for other projects, they choose to enter into more structured partnerships. Programs can provide especially good opportunities to form partnerships with other organizations. Both institutions contribute resources such as mailing lists to use to advertise events, staff to organize and run programs, and funds to pay for supplies, promotion, and presenters.

In 2001, several small history organizations in northwestern Connecticut were interested in adding to their programming schedules and promoting their organizations to residents of each other's communities. As staff of small institutions (the average was two full-time staff at each organization), the members of this group were also looking for the fun that comes from being part of a team. Ten museums, historic sites, and nature centers decided to create a lecture series. Each designated a staff member as its representative on the planning committee. The organizers outlined what each site would do individually and what the planning committee would do together. Eventually settling on a lunchtime format, the group decided to name its program History Bites, with publicity stating, "You supply the lunch, and we supply the drinks and dessert." Each organization agreed to make its mailing list available to the planning committee, to arrange its own lecture in a space at or near its site, and to supply the beverages and sweets. The planning committee members agreed that their respective group's responsibilities were to create and distribute publicity materials, to develop a common evaluation form, and to donate staff time for tasks such as designing the flyer, developing the evaluation instrument, and assembling the mailing.

The program was an overwhelming success. It generated large audiences at each of the sites, persuaded residents of the area's communities to visit cultural institutions in other towns, and gave the planning committee members opportunities to work with their colleagues from other organizations. This last benefit is sometimes overlooked when organizations consider partnerships. In this case, the partnership helped counter the feeling of isolation that comes from working alone or on a very small staff. With such a positive experience, the planners decided to offer another lecture series the following year. Every year, the program evolved a little, as committee members evaluated what had worked well and what had not been so successful.

(continued)

TEXTBOX 5.4 *(Continued)*

They created a theme for each year's lectures, added a modest admission fee—though during the first couple of years, they did not charge visitors to attend—and applied for a small grant to cover costs such as brochure printing and mailing-list management. Now many of the original planning committee members have moved on to other organizations and positions, but the History Bites lecture series endures, continuing to draw large audiences, to build community goodwill for the participating sites, and to allow collaboration among institutions.

When you enter into a partnership, your institution's goals may not be the same as those of the others. Participants do not have to enter into a relationship with identical goals. However, for the collaboration to succeed, each must be honest at the beginning about what it hopes to achieve. Potential partners should assess whether their goals are complementary or whether they conflict (or may conflict in the future) with each other.

Not all partnerships flourish. In some cases, the partners have goals that are too divergent. Sometimes the participants feel that they are contributing or benefiting unequally and become resentful. In some situations, the partnership is a better fit with the mission of one organization than the other. If you are considering a partnership, consult first the many resources on developing effective collaborations. See, for example, chapter 5 in Book 3 of this series. You may also want to consult the "Community Engagement" section of the American Association of Museum's Information Center, a resource for members. The section includes the Amherst H. Wilder Foundation's Collaboration Factors Inventory, a tool "based on 20 factors researchers have identified as influencing the success of a collaboration."

Who Will Present the Content?

If you plan to have any presenters or demonstrators, you must identify these people as soon as possible so that you can secure them for the event. For example, if you are designing a workshop on the basics of family history research around the talents of a volunteer who is an expert in genealogical research, you will want to make sure that you have not scheduled it for the weekend she is planning to attend her college reunion. If your upcoming festival celebrating the Polish heritage of your community will revolve around demonstrations of Polish cooking and lessons in traditional Polish songs, you will not want to find out at the last minute that you are unable to find anyone to lead these activities.

TEXTBOX 5.5

LEADING ACTIVITIES: A QUICK GUIDELINE

If you will lead the activities during your program, make sure that you are well prepared. Practice any speaking portions of the program. Will you introduce a speaker? Decide in advance what you will say, and practice out loud. If you are including a scavenger hunt in the program, ask someone from outside the museum to do a test run for you to find out if the instructions are clear and how long it might take participants to complete the search. When planning craft activities, make the craft yourself. Pay attention to what is difficult, and imagine ways to modify the steps to make the activity easier to complete. Time yourself to find out how long it takes you to do each of the steps. Double or triple the amount of time that it takes you to do the activity to have a sense of how long it will take the participants. This equation is not exact. Be sure to consider the age of the attendees and the level of skill required to make the craft. Think about how to explain each step to the participants. How can you describe what to do most clearly and succinctly? Try to make your instructions both simple and descriptive. For instance, several years ago, when helping schoolchildren hand-dip candles, a staff member at Colonial Pennsylvania Plantation in Delaware County, Pennsylvania, asked the students to form a line in front of her and her vat of hot wax. She gave the students the easy-to-remember directions of "Dip, drip, and take a trip [to the end of the line]." The children immediately learned the simple three-step rhyme and were able to start applying the instructions to their work. With a little thought, you also will be able to break activities into simple steps. If you have time, ask another staff member or a volunteer to do the activity while you practice your coaching skills.

Try not to be daunted by the search for presenters. Your network likely already includes people with a great deal of expertise. If you are planning programming to accompany your upcoming exhibition of quilts, you might want to offer a workshop on making quilted potholders. Canvass your board members and other volunteers to discover if any of them is knowledgeable about quilt making. Ask if they have any friends who are skilled in that area. Look for local quilt guilds.

Before you engage anyone to present at your program, make sure that the person's presentation skills match the needs of the event. Remember that the quality of the person's speaking skills and organization will reflect upon your museum. You should verify that the presenter will do the job well. If you are planning a workshop or a demonstration, make sure that the person has good teaching skills. Find out, for example, if the person has ever taught a quilting class. (The fact that someone has taught is not necessarily an indication that he or she is skilled at teaching, but it is a good starting point!) If you would like to have a lecture on the history of quilts, be careful not to assume that a person who makes them today is an expert on the background of these textiles. A person who has written articles on the history of quilts and quilt making or who has spoken on the subject in the past is a better bet than someone who simply makes beautiful and technically exquisite quilts. Try to find a copy of the person's articles and read them. Ask other organizations that have invited the person to speak how the audience reacted to the presentation.

In some cases, you may start your search for an expert by looking outside of your community. Do silhouettes of the former residents hang in the hall of your historic house museum? You might want to find a silhouette artist to spend an afternoon at your museum cutting silhouettes of visitors. The artist might charge a flat rate for his or her services or a fee for each portrait made. To locate an appropriate person for the job, try an Internet search using the terms that best describe the expertise you are seeking. In this case, you might use the following search terms: "silhouette artist, traditional." If that does not yield the results you want, modify your search by adding or substituting other appropriate words.

Make use of the directories of performers and presenters created by regional and national organizations. Many states have arts and culture organizations that can serve as an excellent resource for you. In Colorado, for example, museum staff can find presenters through a myriad of sources, including the online directories provided by the Colorado Council on the Arts, the Colorado Dance Alliance, the Colorado Folk Arts Council, and Rocky Mountain Storytellers. If you are not sure whether such organizations exist in your area, search the Internet using your state name and key words found in these groups' names. For example, you might search for "Arizona storytelling directory" or "New Jersey arts league." Professional organizations such as the Association for Living History, Farm, and Agricultural Museums (ALHFAM) sometimes keep lists of resources. On ALHFAM's website (www.alhfam.org), for instance, you can search the section called "Products and Services," located in the "Living History Resources" section. In some instances, your museum might want to schedule a presenter through a national group such as Young Audiences, a nonprofit arts organization dedicated to making arts programming available to children. In each of the organization's locations throughout the country, Young Audiences provides a list of performers and serves as a booking agent for each.

If you are looking for someone with scholarly expertise, a literature review is a good place to begin. Try searching the catalog of a good university research library. Look for books relevant to your subject published in the last few years.

If you have access to JSTOR (an online archive of scholarly journals and other material) or a subscription to journals in the field, check them for recent publications. Which journals you consult will depend on the subject of your program, but some likely candidates are *Journal of American History*, *The Public Historian*, *Journal of African American History*, and *American Quarterly*. Some of the book or journal authors you find might live near your site. Investigate the websites of nearby universities to learn about the research specialties of faculty members. Ask people in your museum network if they know of potential speakers. And feel free to approach museum staff at other institutions whom you have not met if you think that they might be able to provide you with ideas.

Finally, always keep your eyes open for potential presenters, even if you are not currently in need of a new one. Newspaper articles, craft fairs, school events, and continuing education course catalogs, to name a few, are all possible sources of experts. Create a file and add names and contact information as you find them. It is hard to predict what your needs might be in a few years, so be expansive in your collecting. Pick up flyers at other museums; bookmark or print Web pages that spark your imagination. You never know what may prove useful.

Identifying potential contributors is just the first step in engaging them to be part of your event. When you contact a prospective presenter, explain exactly what you would like that person to do. Are you asking for a lecture or a demonstration? Will the person lead an activity? Outline the format of the program, indicating whether you will have more than one presenter, the program duration, how long you expect the person to speak, and so forth. Make sure that the contributor knows the target audience and how many people you predict will attend. Be clear about whether you will compensate the person for his or her participation. What form will the remuneration take? Can you provide a stipend? Will you reimburse the person for mileage? Will you pay for lodging or meals? If you do not have cash to use as payment, consider your other options. Would a complimentary annual membership in your organization be an appropriate token of your appreciation?

After you have settled all these details, send a contract to the presenter. Make sure that it confirms the event date and time, what service the presenter will perform, and what the compensation will be. Include your expectations for poor weather. For example, will an outdoor event take place if there is rain? Do you reserve the right to cancel an event in case of snow or other bad weather? Will you partially compensate the person if you cancel only a few hours before the program is scheduled to begin? Remember to include details about who will provide any special equipment. If you are contracting with a musician, make sure you have spelled out who will provide the sound system. Print two copies, sign both, and send them to the presenter. Ask the presenter to add his or her signature to one of the copies and return it to you. See figures 5.1a and 5.1b for a sample confirmation letter and contract.

March 21, 2007

Roberto Garza

Dear Roberto,

We are so pleased that you are available to participate in the Homestead Museum's early California festival on Sunday, May 6. The festival, called *Romance of the Ranchos*, will feature music, historic house tours, demonstrations (adobe making, blacksmithing, wood carving, etc.), and family activities. As I mentioned in my e-mail, we'd like for you to make two presentations as Pio Pico on the steps of the Walter P. Temple Memorial Mausoleum. We will set up a small sound system and clip a microphone to your jacket so that visitors can easily hear your remarks. You can share the same information with visitors at both presentations, or vary them depending on the material you'd like to cover. It would be ideal to have you talk about such topics as the *Ranchito*, Pico's life and friendships, and his feelings about the Mexican-American War and statehood.

Enclosed you will find a contract for the event. At your convenience, please return a copy to me in the enclosed self-addressed, stamped envelope (I included an extra copy for your files). As the event draws nearer, I will send you flyers.

If I can provide you with any additional information, please call me at (626) 968-8492. We look forward to working with you again!

Cordially,

Alexandra Rasic
Public Programs Manager

Enclosures

Figure 5.1a. Sending a confirmation letter to each performer or speaker is an essential part of preparing for an event. (Courtesy of the Homestead Museum, City of Industry, California)

What Sort of Staffing Will the Program Require?

What sort of setup will the program require? Think about whether you will need furniture moved, refreshments prepared, supplies readied, and so on. Next, ask yourself who will accomplish these tasks. How many people will you need to get the work done efficiently?

During the program itself, what will your staffing needs be? If charging participants a fee for the program, you will likely need to station someone at the entrance to accept money or to admit people who have already registered and paid. If you plan to have a written program of events, decide whether you prefer

---

CONTRACT

This is to confirm that Roberto Garza will make two presentations as Pio Pico at the Homestead Museum on Sunday, May 6, 2007, at 1:30 and 3:30 p.m. Roberto Garza will provide all materials needed for his presentations. The Homestead Museum will supply a sound system. Upon completion of this contract, the Homestead Museum will pay Roberto Garza a $------- honorarium. In the event the Homestead Museum cancels their festival for any reason prior to Roberto Garza's arrival on May 6, the Museum's liability shall be limited to 25% of the total fee.

General Conditions

The Contractor will remove all debris so that he/she will leave the site in the same condition in which he/she found it. The Homestead Museum shall designate the appropriate location of disposing of non-hazardous waste.

Any and all equipment brought onto the Homestead Museum premises by the Contractor is present at the Contractor's risk. Such equipment may be inspected for the conformance with the Museum's regulations by the Museum staff. The Homestead Museum shall in no way be responsible for the loss or damage of such equipment.

The Contractor is fully and completely responsible for damage to objects, equipment, and the Museum buildings and grounds, as well as for any injury to themselves, Museum staff, and Museum visitors arising from or incident to the use of the Contractor's equipment and Contractor's acts. The Contractor shall indemnify and hold harmless the City of Industry, the Industry Urban Development Agency, and Historical Resources, Inc., and the officers and employees thereof from, and to defend it or them against, any and all claims, damages, demands, causes of action, liabilities, lawsuits, expenses, and costs whatsoever, including actual attorney's fees, arising out of the Contractor's use of the Homestead Museum premises.

X_____
Roberto Garza   Date

X_____
Karen Graham Wade   Date
President, Historical Resources Inc.
Director, Homestead Museum

Figure 5.1b. Sending a contract to each performer or speaker is an essential part of preparing for an event. (Courtesy of the Homestead Museum, City of Industry, California)

to have someone hand it to participants or have them pick up copies as they walk in. If you are having speakers, someone will need to greet them before the event and later introduce them to the audience. During programs that require participants to move from one area to another, you may need staff to help visitors find their way. If you have planned activity stations, you will likely need a facilitator at each. At the end of the event, you may need someone to distribute evaluations. And finally, there is the inevitable cleanup.

Once you have anticipated your staffing needs, start thinking about how they match your resources. Do you have paid staff available to fill every position?

Is this program better suited to staffing by volunteers? If you plan to use volunteers to help with the program itself, determine whether your current volunteer corps is adequate for the job or you need to recruit new volunteers.

No matter who will do what job for the program, make sure that each helper knows his or her tasks. And make sure that all staff—paid and unpaid—understand the program goals. One way to ensure that all people assisting with the program understand their responsibilities and the objectives of the event is to write an e-mail to each confirming his or her participation and outlining what you are asking the person to do at the event. Be sure to include what time you would like the person to arrive, how long the person will need to stay, what sort of attire you would like him or her to wear, and whether you will provide food. The experience will be more fun for everyone if all parties know what to expect. For example, you do not want someone who is slated to help with a quill-pen-and-ink demonstration to arrive at the event in a brand-new pair of white pants.

Confirmation e-mails and conversations may take care of most of the training needs for staff. However, you may want to hold special training for everyone who will be involved on the day of the program. To make the choice about whether to hold training, think about who will help and what experience these individuals have. People who have assisted with other programs may need minimal instruction. Staff and volunteers who are new to your museum or to programming may benefit from a training session. The complexity level of the event will also contribute to your decision.

How Will You Publicize the Program?

Few small museums have the budget to pay for advertising. If you do number among the lucky few, think carefully about where you will get the most attention from your target audience. Whether or not you are able to pay for advertising, try to make the best use you can of your other publicity options. (See chapter 1 of Book 4 for more information on marketing.) Remembering the often-repeated idea that people need to hear about a program several times before they decide to attend, think of as many different ways as possible to let the public know about your program. You might start by compiling a list of locations throughout the community where you can post flyers for the program. You might find community bulletin boards at grocery stores, community centers, church halls, post offices, and coffee shops. Ask trustees and other volunteers to help distribute flyers to each of the places on your list. (Keep this list from program to program, refining it as you go.) Be sure to post some of those flyers at your own site.

Send a press release to local news outlets, including your town newspaper, the periodicals of other towns and cities in the area, and any local television and radio stations. Be sure that you do not overlook any free weekly papers delivered in your area. And make sure that you contact the local community-access cable station. Press releases are not hard to write, but they do need to be straightforward and follow certain formatting conventions. Many websites offer advice on how to write and format press releases. See, for example, the how-to page on the website of Press Release 365, one of many press release distribution services (www.pressrelease365.com/how-to-write-a-press-release.htm). Contact each of the media outlets you have identified to learn how they would like to receive news. Some may want to receive press releases via facsimile, but most will likely prefer e-mail, possibly with the release attached as a portable document format (PDF) file. Ask what fax number or e-mail address to use for each. Just as with the list of places to post flyers, keep your press release list from program to program. Periodically verify with each place on the list that you still have the correct contact information.

Think about how best to reach the audience you have targeted for this program. A reading of Civil War–era letters from your archives will probably interest Civil War round tables and reenactor groups. Try an online search to identify such organizations. When Gadsby's Tavern Museum began its toddler program, staff searched the Internet for Alexandria, Virginia, moms' groups. The museum found that sending messages to these organizations was its most effective method of publicizing the program. Ask organizations to forward an e-mail invitation or to make an announcement at their next meeting. Brainstorm about other ways to make use of existing networks to distribute program information. For example, some schools will distribute information about family programming to their students. Check with the public and private schools in your area to learn their policies. Remember to include day-care centers and preschools in your research. Ask people who are in your museum's network to help alert others to events through all the means at their disposal. For example, suggest that volunteers who live in condominiums put a notice in their residences' newsletters.

Publicize both by making information available to those who seek it from you and by sending it out to the public. Make sure that everyone who answers the telephone at your museum knows basic information about the event. Prepare a summary sheet listing the event name, date, reservation requirements, cost, minimum or maximum age, and so forth, for each staff member or volunteer who might answer questions about the program. Post the who, what, when, and where, as well as more detailed information, on your organization's website. At the very least, make sure that if you have members, you send them a special invitation to participate. You might also want to invite visitors to register for an events mailing list. Remember when sending e-mail announcements to respect your visitors by including a way for them to opt out of the list.

HistoryBites

Letters & Diaries

* All lectures are at noon on **Thursdays.**
  Bring lunch. Beverages & desserts are provided.
  Please contact the hosting organization for
  directions and more information.
  Reservations requested, but not required.
  Suggested donation: $2 per lecture

✳ March 25, 2010
Life on the Farm
Joe Shupenis, town historian
Uncover the daily lives of Bethlehem farmers in the early 1900s
through an exploration of their journals.
Old Bethlem Historical Society
(203) 266-5188, www.ci.bethlehem.ct.us
LECTURE SITE: Johnson Memorial Hall of Christ,
Episcopal Church, Main Street South, Bethlehem, CT

✳ April 1, 2010
A First Archaeological Expedition to Afghanistan
Henry Hart, local Woodbury resident
Memories of the 1949 American Museum Of Natural History
expedition to Afghanistan.
Old Woodbury Historical Society
(203) 263-2446
LECTURE SITE: Woodbury Senior Center, Woodbury, CT

✳ April 8, 2010
Fred and Jennie: A Civil War Love Story
Ernest Barker, local author
This living history performance features readings from the Civil
War letters between Frederick A. Lucas, who served in the 2nd
CT Heavy Artillery and his future wife, Sarah Jane Wadhams.
Torrington Historical Society
(860) 482-8260, www.torringtonhistoricalsociety.org
192 Main Street, Torrington, CT

✳ April 15, 2010
A 19th Century Love Affair
John Alter, Gunnery teacher & Sarah Griswold, assistant curator
Explore the life & times of Gunnery School founder, Frederick
Gunn, & his fiance Abigail Brinsmade through their personal
correspondence during his exile in Towanda, PA.
Gunn Memorial Library & Museum
(860) 868-7756, www.gunnlibrary.org
5 Wykeham Road, On the Green, Washington, CT

✳ April 22, 2010
Reading Between the Lines
Julie Frey, curator, Litchfield Historical Society
Reflections on the craftsmen's advertisements and journals
of early nineteenth century Litchfield.
Litchfield Historical Society
(860) 567-4501, www.litchfieldhistoricalsociety.org
LECTURE SITE: Litchfield History Museum, 7 South Street,
Litchfield, CT

✳ April 29, 2010
Personal Writing, Public Events
Gerald Gecl, educator and guide, Topsmead
Discover how the journal entries, letters & other correspon-
dence of Edith Morton Chase intersect with worldly affairs.
Topsmead State Forest
(860) 567-5694, www.dep.state.ct.us/rec/parks/ctforests.htm
LECTURE SITE: Litchfield Community Center, 421 Bantam
Road, (US 202), Litchfield, CT

✳ May 6, 2010
Letters from Paris...and Naugatuck
Ann Y. Smith, past curator and director of the Mattatuck
Revelations on the personal insights that letters can bring to
larger historical narratives, specifically revealed through the
personal letters of the art collecting Whittemore family.
Mattatuck Museum Arts and History Center
(203) 753-0381 ext. 10 www.mattatuckmuseum.org
144 West Main St., Waterbury, CT

✳ May 13, 2010
Making A Personal Connection to the Lives of Our Forefathers
Timothy Beard, genealogist and author
Explorations on family roots of New Englanders from
journals, letters & diaries.
Glebe House Museum & The Gertrude Jekyll Garden
(203) 263-2855 www.theglebehouse.org
LECTURE SITE: Woodbury Senior Center, Woodbury, CT

✳ May 20, 2010
Natalie Van Fleck
Marc Chabot, archivist Flanders Nature Center
Reflections on artist, farmer and environmentalist, Natalie
Van Fleck from the perspective of her diaries and oral
histories.
Flanders Nature Center & Pomeraug River Watershed Coalition
(203) 263-3711, www.flandersnaturecenter.org
LECTURE SITE: Sugar House at Flanders Nature Center

✳ May 27, 2009
Revelations Through Letters
Kristin Havill, site administrator, Bellamy-Ferriday
Discover the life and times of the Reverend Joseph
Bellamy through an examination of his letters.
The Bellamy-Ferriday House & Garden
(203) 266-7596 www.ctlandmarks.org
LECTURE SITE: First Church of Bethlehem, Bethlehem, CT

Figure 5.2. Brochures that can be mailed or posted remain an effective publicity tool for many organizations, even in the digital age. (Courtesy of History Bites partners, Connecticut)

What Supplies Will You Need to Run Your Program?

Most programs require supplies of some sort. Start with the publicity and think through every part of the event to determine what you will need.

1. Will you mail invitations or program announcements? Will you work with a printer or will you make them in-house. If you will make them yourself, do you have the appropriate kind and amount of paper?

2. Will you have a check-in table at the door? Do you want to cover it with a tablecloth? Make sure that you have a table and a chair or two ready. Prepare a cash box with small bills and coins. Will you give tickets or write receipts? If people have registered, make sure you include at the table the list of attendees. Organize it alphabetically or in some other way that is logical for your event.

3. If you are sponsoring a craft activity, what materials will you need? Do you have enough for each table? Do you have enough table seating for all the participants? Do you have child-friendly supplies? For example, are you offering glue sticks instead of liquid glue to young children? Do you have scissors with rounded tips?

4. If you are holding a symposium, do you have a list of speakers and a list of attendees ready? Are there any handouts to distribute? Do you want to place all these in folders before the event?

5. If you are organizing games, what materials will you need? Do you have enough for several groups to play at one time?

6. Do you need signs directing participants to the correct entrance or part of the building?

7. Do you plan to distribute programs? If so, and if you have mailed event announcements, do you want them to match in paper and design?

8. Will you need a digital projector or a slide projector? A computer? What about a screen? A flip chart or a dry-erase board?

9. Will you need extension cords?

10. Will any of the activities be messy? Do you need to have wet wipes available?

11. Do any of the participants need to be identified in any way? Do you need name tags? If you are having a competition, do you want to designate the judges with sashes or stickers?

12. Will you serve refreshments? When will you make them available? Do you have enough serving dishes and utensils? Do you have adequate napkins, plates, cups, and cutlery?

13. Do you have plenty of trash containers, and are they in the most convenient locations?
14. Do you have any necessary prizes ready? Will you need door prizes, awards, or favors?
15. Will cleanup require anything special? Do you need extra trash bags or cleaning products? Will you need containers for extra food?

Will Your Program Include Food?

The topic of food comes up frequently as people plan programs. Make sure that you have thought carefully about refreshments and your event. If you are hosting an outdoor concert, may audience members bring food with them? Do you want to advertise picnicking as part of the fun? Will you provide trash containers, or will attendees be responsible for carrying out whatever they bring in?

Sometimes museums sell food as part of a program. Selling food often necessitates following local health department guidelines. Make sure that you have all the information you need about these requirements if you are considering making refreshments available for participants to purchase. If you are using a caterer, this professional firm should have all the necessary health permits. You may also need to consider permits if you are having alcohol at your event. Check your state's regulations to find out when or if you need a license for alcohol distribution. Remember to apply for any necessary permits in plenty of time.

At other events, museums provide food as part of the program. In some of these cases, museum staff and volunteers organize the food. For instance, a Mother's Day tea might include finger sandwiches and pastries made by a committee of volunteers. A lecture might end with cookies and lemonade obtained from the local grocery store. Other programs might require the services of a caterer. At a daylong symposium, museum staff might provide professionally made box lunches.

In some instances, food is the event. The President Benjamin Harrison Home joins forces with another Indianapolis historic house museum, the Morris-Butler House Museum, to offer "Stroll into Spring: A Progressive Dinner." During this event, participants visit six houses in the museums' neighborhood. At each home, diners eat one course of their meal. The program has many benefits. It ties the museums to their part of the city, brings new visitors each year to each, and builds a feeling of community among the residents and museums. In addition, the program serves as a fundraiser for both museums.

No matter what method you use to obtain the food for your event, make sure you think through the logistics related to refreshments:

- How will you get the food to your site? Will someone on staff pick it up, or will it be delivered?
- Where will you keep the food until you are ready for it?
- Will you need the food to be arranged on serving dishes? If so, who will do that job?
- Will you need extra trash cans?
- Will you set out food for people to pick up as they wish, or will you need someone to serve the refreshments?
- If you need any permits or licenses, who will pick them up?
- Who will clean up?

When planning for programs with food, museums must also consider the special requirements of their collections and buildings. If you intend to have refreshments inside at your space, you will want to think about any limitations you need to place on food consumption in order to protect your collections. Some museums require that visitors keep food and beverages outside of exhibition areas. To remind visitors not to take such items into galleries, staff place tables for cups and plates at the entrance to each exhibition space. Other museums choose to allow refreshments into galleries in which all objects are in cases. Most museums restrict the kinds of food and drinks that may be consumed, no matter where the eating and drinking will take place. Red wine and messy, drippy foods are generally on the list of forbidden items. You will want to develop your own policies before you host events with food (and before someone splashes red wine or cranberry juice on the turn-of-the-century wedding gown in your new special exhibition).

Do You Have Contingency Plans?

Bad weather can wreak havoc with a program. Decide ahead of time what you will do if a snowstorm occurs on the day of your event. Some museums publicize that they follow the area school system's response to snow. If school is canceled, then so is the program. Discuss whether you need another method for letting participants know that a program is canceled. If attendees must register in advance, call each or send an e-mail as soon as you know of a change in plans. If you are not requiring registration, you might want to ask local radio and television stations to announce the cancelation. No matter what other system you use, make sure that your website and telephone message include up-to-date status information. Have a plan that spells out who will decide whether to cancel the program, how program staff and volunteers will learn of the decision, who will contact the registered participants, and who will make the changes on the website and outgoing answering machine or voice mail message (and how to make the changes). If you decide to postpone rather than cancel an event, offer that information to prospective participants. When predictions for snow suggest that a program might need to be canceled, make sure that someone takes home all the telephone numbers and e-mail addresses necessary for canceling the event.

Rain and outdoor programs are another difficult combination. When planning an outdoor program, decide what your rain policy will be. Will you hold the program in the rain? Do you want (or can you afford) to rent a tent for the program? Can you find and reserve an indoor space to use as a backup? Make sure that you include rainy-day information in the publicity materials, and make sure that any presenters know the plan.

Imagine that you need to evacuate the building on the day of the program. Do you know where all the emergency exits are? Are there fire extinguishers, and do you know how to use them? Keep a well-stocked first aid kit, and make sure that it is readily accessible.

What Costs Are Associated with the Program and Where Will You Find the Money?

Just as you have thought through all the other aspects of planning the program, consider how much the event will cost. Each aspect of the program, from the publicity to the supplies, may require financial resources. Before you commit to running the event, write down how much you expect to spend on printing, mailings, compensation of presenters, facility rental, supplies, food, and decorations. How much time will it take to plan and hold the program? How much salary money does that represent? School programs can entail additional costs. Your museum might supply pre- and post-visit activities for teachers to use in their classrooms. Some museums hire consultants to write these activities. Many schools have difficulty paying for the buses that they need to transport students to museums for field trips. In response, some institutions provide bus scholarships for schools.

After determining all the costs, identify potential sources of funding. Can your annual budget support the program, or do you need to find other funding? Is grant funding available for this kind of activity? As you try to answer that question, remember that local and state foundations can be fruitful sources of program funding. So can family foundations. (For more information on applying for grants, see publications such as David G. Bauer's *The "How To" Grants Manual: Successful Grant Seeking Techniques for Obtaining Public and Private Grants*, 7th ed. [Lanham, MD: Rowman & Littlefield Publishers, 2011]). Perhaps a business is willing to underwrite the cost of the event. Your board members might have contacts who would help your institution find sponsors.

Do be careful, when asking businesses to support events, that you do not match programs with inappropriate funders. For example, many museums would balk at having an alcohol-related business associated with a children's program. Perhaps you do not need outside funding. Can you structure the program so that participation fees pay all costs except those related to the staff time needed for planning and implementation?

Ideally, a museum will know if it has received outside funding for a program early in the planning stages. In many cases, though, staff must continue planning without knowing if the museum will receive a grant or a hoped-for sponsorship will materialize. Ask yourself whether it is possible to run the program without the outside funding. Consider how it must be modified in this case.

How Will You Measure the Program's Success?

Think back to the section that focused on what you want to achieve with this program. Revisit your goals, and ask yourself how you will determine whether you have achieved them. Think about both your institution's goals and your educational goals for your visitors. Ask yourself what questions or observations will most help you to assess your programs' success on multiple levels. For example, you might want to think about what measures will allow you to evaluate whether the program is a success from the perspective of the institution ("Did we teach the historical idea that was the focus of the program?"), the community ("Did the program demonstrate that the museum has value within the community?"), and the participants ("Did attendees have opportunities to try something new and to socialize?").

Perhaps you have decided that you have two goals for a hearth cooking class. You want participants to be able to compare foods that were common in the late eighteenth century to today's counterparts, and you want to raise money for your institution. During your program you might prepare eighteenth-century recipes and then serve each with a modern equivalent. Success might come about if the program attendees discuss with each other and the demonstrator their reactions to the paired foods. You can gather data by observing and recording unsolicited comments or by actively asking visitors to describe similarities and differences between the two dishes. Both of these techniques will enable you to evaluate whether you have met your first goal. To gauge whether you have reached your second goal, you need to have decided as you were planning the program how much money you would like to earn. When the program is finished and you have paid all the bills, you will know if you have accomplished this objective. For each of these goals, remember to establish the criteria for assessing your success before the program begins so that you can know what to look for, measure, or track during the program itself.

Executing

What Do You Need to Do on the Day of the Program?

All volunteers and employees who will help with the program should already know what they are going to be doing at the event. You can make the program run smoothly by devising one-page reference sheets for each of them. These sheets might include a schedule of events, the name of the person to contact if there is an emergency or minor crisis, a reminder of the goals of the event (e.g., we want everyone to have fun; participants should gain insight into the lives of people during the Great Depression), and so forth. People who will be taking money should have a reminder of the ticket costs. Helpers who will be running interactive activities should have written instructions on how to do the activity and suggestions for how to talk with visitors about the connections between the activity and the theme or message of the program. If staff will rotate through different posts, make sure that everyone has the rotation schedule. Also, make sure that the person in charge of the event is not the only one who knows how to respond to any issues that arise. The greater the number of people who know the details of the program schedule and other logistics, the more likely it is that a knowledgeable person will be on hand to solve a problem when it happens.

When assigning jobs, remember to designate someone to meet any outside presenters. Try to reserve one person to float; this person can give other staff members breaks when needed, offer an extra pair of hands if a problem crops up, and generally serve as a troubleshooter. If another staff person becomes ill or is otherwise unable to attend, you can replace the missing employee or volunteer with the floater. Setup helpers will need to post any necessary signage. When planning for signage, think of all the places you think you will need directional or informational signs. Then add more. Setup helpers will also make sure furniture is in the correct location and place supplies wherever they are needed. Cleanup helpers will ensure that the event space is returned to its preprogram state.

Expect that something will not go as planned. Successful program management requires adaptability. Try to anticipate what could go wrong and have solutions ready. But do not be thrown when something you did not expect happens. Sometimes surprises are a good sign. For example, if you planned to have fifteen minutes of questions after a speaker's prepared remarks, but the audience and speaker seem intensely engaged in discussion at the end of the designated time, you might choose to let the discussion continue for a little while longer.

Accept that no matter how well you plan, something will go wrong. You cannot control every piece of the program, but you can control your reactions to whatever happens. Try to project a calm and pleasant demeanor. Your attitude as you deal with a situation will greatly influence the way that other staff and participants react. Be resourceful. Most of all, have fun. Remember that you will have a heightened sense of mistakes made and problems with the program, as you are the one who has been planning every detail. For example, the participants are unlikely to know the precise schedule to which you are hoping to adhere. Unless you announce that you are making schedule adjustments as you go, they will assume that the program is unfolding as it was meant to.

Make sure that throughout the program you implement your evaluation plan. For example, if you decided to record the kinds of family discussions that occurred as parents and children worked together to build gingerbread houses, then assign a volunteer or staff member to document this information. If you decided to distribute a questionnaire to participants, then make sure that you leave time to distribute the evaluations, have pencils or pens available, and designate a place for people to return the completed forms. At the end of the program, before you move on to cleaning up, meet briefly with the others who helped at the event to capture everyone's immediate sense of what went well and what did not. At the National Postal Museum in Washington, DC, staff frame this discussion as "keep/change" and use their impressions to start thinking about what elements of a program they might keep for next time and which they might change if they were to offer in the future an event with a similar format, audience, or content.

Assessing

Did the Program Go Well?

Evaluating the program is the first step to planning your next program. Use your experience with this program to help you think about how you want to develop future events. Create a mental or physical checklist to review both the logistics and the details of the learning experience. Write down your reflections. You will likely want to ask yourself the following questions:

- Did the participants learn what you hoped or have the experience that you planned for them?
- How well attended was the program? (Did you have empty seats or have to turn people away?)
- Was the venue size appropriate? Did the facility offer the features you needed for the program activities?
- Did the intended audience show up? Did any other demographic groups participate?
- How did the program fit with the needs, interests, and expectations of the attendees?
- Did the logistics run smoothly? What could have worked better?

- Were there any surprises? What can you learn from them?
- Did the program meet your institutional goals, and is it worth repeating in this format?
- Even if you do not plan to hold this program again, did any elements work so well that you would like to adapt them to other events?
- How will you do things differently next time you hold a program?

There are many ways to gather information about the program. As the section on creating an evaluation plan suggests, you may want to distribute a questionnaire to participants, asking them how they felt about the event. You will certainly want to record your own observations and reactions and seek feedback from others who helped staff the program. If you have any outside presenters, be sure to solicit their observations and reactions to the program and to the participants' experience of it.

Think about whether the format was a success. If you asked people how they learned about the program, can you draw any conclusions about what publicity methods worked best? What adjustments would you make for next time? When Gadsby's Tavern Museum started the Tavern Toddlers program, the staff offered a snack to the participating children. Subsequently, the refreshments were discontinued as staff realized that all the caregivers who attended brought their own snacks. There was no need for the museum to provide food. In fact, some parents prefer to choose what snacks their children eat.

Perhaps the most important question to reflect on after concluding a program is whether the event gained more for your museum than it cost the institution. Done well, programs do one or more of the following: increase visitation, further the educational goals of the museum, earn income, or enhance the organization's reputation. Even if your program meets some of its goals, it might not be a success if it does not meet all of them. A program that attracts a large audience and increases visitation but distracts from the mission is not a good fit. And an elaborate program that beautifully teaches the museum's content but attracts only a handful of participants is a drain on resources that could be used in other ways. As a steward of your museum, it is your responsibility to examine programs and make hard decisions about whether it is wise to continue holding them. Think about the program that attracts a large audience. Is there any way that you can change the theme or focus to capitalize on a successful format but make the content mission oriented? If another program meets your content goals perfectly but does not attract enough visitors to justify the expense it entails, investigate whether you can change the time the event is held or publicize it in a different way. If you are not able to fix a program so that it is aligned with your mission and makes good use of your resources, eliminate it from your calendar of events. Be aware, also, that no program has an unlimited life span. Changes in society, your community, and your institution can render a once great fit a poor option for your museum. For example, during the 2000s, as concerns about student safety and growing budget deficits have grown, school policies around the country have shifted. Many school districts have placed new restrictions on field trips, and some museums that credited a substantial portion of their visitation to students participating in school programs have been badly hurt. These organizations have had to adapt quickly to changing circumstances to survive. Whether you abandon a much-loved program because it no longer represents a good match for your museum or because circumstances force the change, the world of program possibilities is vast, and there are many waiting for you and your museum.

TEXTBOX 5.6

PROGRAM MANAGEMENT CHECKLIST

Planning
- Determine the audience.
- Set institutional objectives and educational goals.
- Choose a format.
- Develop the schedule.
- Select presenters.
- Decide on a staffing plan.
- Plan the publicity.
- Create a supply list.
- Make a contingency plan.
- Develop a budget and determine funding sources.
- Decide on an evaluation plan.

Executing
- Train staff.
- Set up (signs, seating, supplies, etc.).
- Hold the program.
- Clean up.

Assessing
- Gather feedback.
- Analyze data to measure program outcomes against goals and objectives.
- Record thoughts for next time.

What Steps Do You Need to Take to Wrap Up the Program?

Your responsibilities are not finished once the last visitor leaves and the last crumb is cleaned up. If you received funding from a granting agency, you probably have a report to write and submit. Any volunteer who contributed time should receive a thank-you note. Make sure you also thank all funders and sponsors. And if you think you will hold the program again, you will want to write notes to make next year's program planning easier. Jot down thoughts about what went well, what could be improved, and how reality differed from projections. Did you use all the supplies that you purchased? Should you buy more or fewer next year? Review the planning notes to make sure you've captured all the final details. Compose a memo for the program file to make sure that someone else could easily hold the program again.

Successful programs are more than fun events. And successful program management entails more than making sure that each event runs smoothly. Individually and as a group, a museum's programs advance the mission of the institution. Periodically take time out to look at the year's calendar. Create a map of the groups served by the varying programs, as well as the goals, cost, and format of each and the times of day you offer it. Then assess the whole. Consider whether your programming calendar allows you to meet your goals. For instance, are you reaching all the audiences you hope to serve? Are you truly advancing your mission?

As you can see, programs require a lot of thought and hard work. But without them, many museums would not survive. Programs remind the community that we exist. They draw in new faces and offer creative ways for us to achieve our missions. They raise funds that we need to keep our doors open. A well-conceived and -executed program of events will help make your museum an integral part of your community. To make your programs as effective as possible, you need to reexamine them periodically. Take this opportunity to think about what programs you have offered in the past and to imagine the possibilities for the future. The rewards can be enormous.

INDEX

ABOUT THE EDITORS

Cinnamon Catlin-Legutko has worked in the small museum world since 1994 and was the director of the General Lew Wallace Study & Museum in Crawfordsville, Indiana, from 2003 to 2009. In 2008, the museum was awarded the National Medal for Museum Service. Her contributions to the field include leadership of the AASLH Small Museums Committee, service as an IMLS grant reviewer and AAM MAP peer reviewer, and service as an AASLH Council member. She is now CEO of the Abbe Museum in Bar Harbor, Maine.

Stacy Klingler currently serves local history organizations as the assistant director of local history services at the Indiana Historical Society. She began her career in museums as the assistant director of two small museums, before becoming director of the Putnam County Museum in Greencastle, Indiana. She chairs the AASLH's Small Museums Committee (2008–2012) and attended the Seminar for Historical Administration in 2006. While she lives in the history field, her passion is encouraging a love of learning in any environment.

ABOUT THE CONTRIBUTORS

Stephen G. Hague is currently the Society of Architectural Historians of Great Britain Ernest Cook Trust Research Student at Linacre College, University of Oxford, England. His research interests center on architecture, material culture, and social history in the eighteenth-century British Atlantic world. Previously he worked as executive director of Stenton, a historic house museum in Philadelphia administered by the National Society of the Colonial Dames of America in the Commonwealth of Pennsylvania. He holds a master's in history from the University of Virginia and a bachelor's from Binghamton University.

Laura C. Keim is curator of Stenton and Wyck, two house museums located in historic Germantown, as well as a lecturer in historic interiors at Philadelphia University. A graduate of the Winterthur Program in Early American Culture, she holds a preservation degree from the University of Pennsylvania and a bachelor's in art history from Smith College. She has published widely on early American material culture and coauthored Stenton's interpretive plan.

Madeline C. Flagler completed her bachelor's at the University of North Carolina, Chapel Hill, and her graduate studies at the University of Hawaii, Manoa. Previously she has been education director at Mission Houses Museum, Honolulu, Hawaii, and Bellamy Mansion Museum, Wilmington, North Carolina. She is currently executive director at the Wrightsville Beach Museum of History. Each of these is a small museum with limited staff heavily supplemented by volunteers.

Teresa Goforth holds a master's in history from Michigan State University. She teaches museum studies at Michigan State University and Central Michigan University and is an exhibit developer for the consulting firm Museum Explorer, Inc. Formerly the director of a small museum, she was also part, for five years, of the Museum on Main Street team, a joint project between the Smithsonian Institution Traveling Exhibition Service and the Federation of State Humanities Councils.

Eugene Dillenburg has been an exhibit developer for more than twenty years: the Field Museum of Natural History (1989–1997); the Shedd Aquarium (1997–2001); the Science Museum of Minnesota (2001–present); and also assorted freelance.

Janice Klein has over twenty-five years of museum experience, including ten as registrar at the Field Museum, Chicago, and eight as executive director of the Mitchell Museum of the American Indian (Evanston, Illinois). She currently runs her own consulting company, EightSixSix Consulting, which specializes in collections management and small museum administration. She has organized numerous professional workshops and conference sessions on issues ranging from the computerization of collections to public relations for small museums.

Rebecca Martin is a museum educator in Washington, DC. Her small museum experience includes spending seven years at the Litchfield Historical Society in Litchfield, Connecticut, and serving on the board of the Connecticut League of History Organizations. She studied in the history and museum studies programs at Grinnell College and the University of Delaware. She is passionate about developing ways to help all visitors learn from and enjoy their museum experiences.